NTC
Vocabulary Builders

Red Book

Peter Fisher, Editorial Consultant
National-Louis University

 **National Textbook Company**
a division of *NTC Publishing Group* • Lincolnwood, Illinois USA

Acknowledgments

The pronunciation key used in the flash cards has been reprinted by permission from the AMERICAN HERITAGE DICTIONARY OF THE ENGLISH LANGUAGE, THIRD EDITION, copyright © 1992 by Houghton Mifflin Company.

Cover Illustration: Sandie Burton
Cover Design: Ophelia Chambliss
Editorial Development: Cottage Communications

Published by National Textbook Company, a division of NTC Publishing Group.

Library of Congress Catalog Card Number: 94-65413

4 5 6 7 8 9 0 VL 9 8 7 6 5 4 3 2 1

Contents

Name _____

The Surrender Speech of Chief Joseph

It has been called the outstanding example of Native American oratory. Its simplicity and expressiveness stand in sharp contrast to the **harangues** so commonly delivered by orators of the late nineteenth century.

5 Chief Joseph had led hundreds of Nez Perce men, women, and children on a 1,500-mile **trek** over mountains and rivers in the winter of 1877. Driven from their home along the Snake River, these native inhabitants of present-day Idaho and Oregon sought the safety of Canada. However, just a few miles from the Canadian border, the Nez Perce were attacked by United States troops led by General Nelson Appleton Miles.

10 Facing the total **annihilation** of his sick and exhausted people, Chief Joseph accepted the promise of General Miles that the Nez Perce would be returned to their home if they surrendered. Chief Joseph spoke the following words to his people:

I am tired of fighting. Our chiefs are killed. Looking Glass is
15 dead. The old men are all dead.

It is the young men who say no and yes. He who led the young men is dead. It is cold and we have no blankets. The little children are freezing to death. My people, some of them have run away to the hills and have no blankets—no food. No one knows where they are—perhaps they are freezing to death.
20

I want to have time to look for my children and see how many of them I can find. Maybe I shall find them among the dead. Hear me, my chiefs, I am tired, my heart is sad and sick. From where the sun now stands, I will fight no more forever.

25 This brief but **eloquent** speech by Chief Joseph is considered one of the most moving and memorable in American literature. In a few sincere and moving sentences, it **succinctly** expressed the suffering and **anguish** of the Native American and the **ferocity** of war.

In the end, General Miles's promise was only a **ruse.** Chief Joseph and
30 the surviving Nez Perce were not allowed to return. Until his death in 1904, Chief Joseph **petitioned** the U.S. government repeatedly to allow the Nez Perce to return to their ancestral home, but his pleas were met with **indifference.** The Nez Perce never saw their home again.

Words
anguish
annihilation
eloquent
ferocity
harangue
indifference
petition
ruse
succinct
trek

Each word in this lesson's word list appears in dark type in the selection you just read. Think about how the vocabulary word is used in the selection, then write the letter for the best answer to each question.

1. A *harangue* (line 2) can best be described as _____ .   1. _____
   (A) quiet thoughtfulness   (B) a clever speech
   (C) a cruel trick   (D) a long, wordy speech

2. A *trek* (line 5) is a(n) _____ .   2. _____
   (A) sea voyage   (B) wilderness trail
   (C) long, difficult trip   (D) adventure

3. Which word could best replace *annihilation* in line 10?   3. _____
   (A) starvation   (B) release
   (C) destruction   (D) rejection

4. Which word could best replace *eloquent* in line 25?   4. _____
   (A) complex   (B) expressive
   (C) musical   (D) loud

5. A *succinct* speech (line 27) is one that is _____ .   5. _____
   (A) short and to the point   (B) confusing
   (C) historic   (D) convincing

6. Which word or words could best replace *anguish* in line 27?   6. _____
   (A) agony   (B) cooperative spirit
   (C) hostility   (D) stupidity

7. Which word could best replace *ferocity* in line 28?   7. _____
   (A) gallantry   (B) wisdom
   (C) excitement (D) savagery

8. Which word or words could best replace *ruse* in line 29?   8. _____
   (A) trick   (B) insult
   (C) solemn promise (D) courtesy

9. Which word or words could best replace *petitioned* in line 31?   9. _____
   (A) visited   (B) asked
   (C) attacked (D) prayed to

10. Which word or words could best replace *indifference* in line 33?   10. _____
    (A) unconcern   (B) enthusiasm
    (C) agreement   (D) strange behavior

Applying Meaning

Follow the directions below to write a sentence using a vocabulary word.

1. Describe a sporting event you have seen or would like to see. Use any form of the word *annihilate*.

   _____

   _____

   _____

2. Describe a speech or sermon. Use any form of the word *harangue*.

   _____

   _____

   _____

3. Tell how you feel about something or someone. Use any form of the word *indifference*.

   _____

   _____

   _____

4. Describe a trip you or someone you know took. Use any form of the word *trek*.

   _____

   _____

   _____

5. Tell how your class might go about asking the principal for a special favor. Use any form of the word *petition*.

   _____

   _____

   _____

Read each sentence or short passage below. Write "correct" on the answer line if the vocabulary word has been used correctly. Write "incorrect" on the answer line if the vocabulary word has been used incorrectly.

6. Even though the question was long and complicated, the teacher gave a very *succinct* answer.

   6. _____

7. The banquet table was set with the most *eloquent* dishes.

   7. _____

8. The contest turned out to be just a *ruse* for getting people to visit the store.

8. _____

9. I wrote a *petition* to Aunt Mary thanking her for my birthday present.

9. _____

10. The storm struck with a *ferocity* never before seen in that part of the country.

10. _____

11. The *anguish* caused by the sudden death of her pet took years to overcome.

11. _____

12. When he did not return my phone calls or answer my letters, I decided that he was *indifferent* about the proposal.

12. _____

13. I considered his annoying stares to be very inappropriate. I do not want this kind of *haranguing* while I am working.

13. _____

14. In trying to find the perfect college, we ended up *trekking* around the entire country.

14. _____

For each word used incorrectly, write a sentence using the word properly.

_____

_____

_____

_____

_____

_____

_____

_____

_____

_____

_____

_____

Mastering Meaning

Think about the events surrounding Chief Joseph's surrender speech. If you had been a newspaper reporter observing the surrender, how would you describe what you saw and heard? Write an article for your newspaper about what happened that day in 1877 near the Canadian border. Include a headline. Use some of the words you studied in this lesson.

Lesson 2 Part A

Name _____

How many speakers have you heard in your lifetime? You have no doubt heard speakers and speeches that left you bored and weary. A few may have changed the way you thought or may have moved you to take some action. There are as many types and styles of speeches as there are speakers. In this lesson you will learn ten words that describe speakers and how they speak.

Unlocking Meaning

Read the sentences or short passages below. Write the letter for the correct definition of the italicized vocabulary word.

Even though the subject was complicated and difficult, the teacher was quite *articulate* in her explanation. By the end of the period, everyone understood the problem.

  1. (A) able to express thoughts well
     (B) argumentative
     (C) often misunderstood
     (D) loud and talkative

The captain's defiant call for action was only *bravado*. When the fighting started, he was nowhere to be found.

  2. (A) a deep sense of courage and commitment
     (B) mechanical
     (C) showy behavior without courage behind it
     (D) a very interesting speech

No one was fooled by the newspaper's *effusive* praise of the football coach. Everyone knows Coach Riley is the editor's brother-in-law.

  3. (A) disguised
     (B) excessive; gushing
     (C) commonplace; ordinary
     (D) moving and sincere

Arthur's *garrulous* behavior at the party caused many people to leave early. Once he gets started there is no stopping him. After a while your ears start to hurt.

  4. (A) excessively talkative
     (B) quiet and shy
     (C) embarrassing
     (D) cordial and engaging

Words

articulate

bravado

effusive

garrulous

glib

histrionics

laconic

polemic

trite

verbosity

1. _____

2. _____

3. _____

4. _____

The politician's *glib* response to my question convinced me she would not get my vote. That subject is far too important to be dismissed with such a simple answer.

5. (A) intelligent and perceptive
   (B) impressive
   (C) untruthful
   (D) superficial and insincere

5. _____

When the candidate held up the flag and tearfully reminded us that he was a veteran, the audience began to feel uneasy. Such *histrionics* do not usually get votes.

6. (A) powerful arguments
   (B) childish behavior
   (C) excessive emotional appeals
   (D) patriotism

6. _____

It is hard to believe that Phil, one of the most talkative and friendly people in school, has such a *laconic* brother.

7. (A) speaking briefly and to the point
   (B) angry and hostile
   (C) dull and lazy
   (D) foolish

7. _____

I hated to see Roberto take his seat in the auditorium. He was certain to engage the speaker in some *polemic*. No matter what her opinion might be, Roberto was certain to take the opposite view.

8. (A) unusual behavior
   (B) controversy or argument
   (C) lengthy discussion
   (D) false praise

8. _____

I had hoped to hear something fresh and interesting at last night's career forum. However, in the end the speakers offered the same *trite* advice I have heard again and again: Stay in school. Study hard. Good things will start to happen.

9. (A) exciting and interesting
   (B) humorous
   (C) logical; sensible
   (D) overused; meaningless

9. _____

Jackie bragged about having written the longest term paper in the class. It was twice as long as the assignment required. If the teacher gives grades for *verbosity*, Jackie will get an A.

10. (A) wordiness
    (B) sincerity
    (C) humility
    (D) neatness

10. _____

Applying Meaning

Read each sentence or short passage below. Write "correct" on the answer line if the vocabulary word has been used correctly. Write "incorrect" on the answer line if the vocabulary word has been used incorrectly.

1. In their day, Benjamin Franklin's proverbs were considered quite clever, but after more than two hundred years, they have become some of the *tritest* expressions in the language.

   1. _____

2. Because it was late and we were all eager to get home, we asked the speaker to give a *verbose* answer to the final question.

   2. _____

3. It is little wonder that Colonel Stern is so greatly admired. His *bravado* is apparent in every speech.

   3. _____

4. Her ability to *articulate* how we all felt about the problem made Juanita the obvious choice for chairperson.

   4. _____

5. Ruben shook everyone's hand vigorously as he greeted each guest *effusively*.

   5. _____

6. His *garrulous* manner made conversation difficult. Every question or comment got a one-word answer.

   6. _____

7. Political advertisements prove nothing. The ten-second sound bite can provide only *glib* answers to complex problems.

   7. _____

8. The movie cowboy was often a man of few words. He was portrayed *laconically* answering "yup" or "nope" to every question someone asked.

   8. _____

9. Maria's *polemics* made her unpopular with the audience. Everyone had come to hear the mayor's proposals, not Maria's constant objections.

   9. _____

10. Next year my brother will receive his degree in *histrionics*. He has done a great deal of research on the French Revolution.

    10. _____

11. We were not sure that the ring was a genuine antique. It might be a cleverly done *articulate*.

    11. _____

12. In the distance we saw a faint *glib* of sunlight shining through the thick forest.

    12. _____

For each word used incorrectly, write a sentence using the word properly.

_____

_____

_____

_____

_____

_____

_____

_____

_____

_____

_____

_____

_____

_____

_____

_____

_____

Cultural Literacy Note

Silence Is Golden

There is a popular proverb that says, "Silence is golden. Speech is silver." It suggests that while speech is admirable, complete silence can be more valuable. Do you agree?

Cooperative Learning: Work with a partner to list some situations in which silence is preferable to speaking. Are there times at school or at home when the more you talk, the worse things become? List some ways of talking that get you into trouble, like glib answers or histrionic outbursts. Use words from this lesson.

Name _____

One of the most easily recognized Latin roots is *-bell-,* which comes from the Latin word *bellum,* meaning "war." The Latin word *caedere* means "to cut" or "to kill." This root often appears in English words as *-cis-* or *-cid-.* Another Latin word, *vincere,* means "to conquer" or "defeat" and usually appears as *-vinc-* in English words. However, it can also appear in other forms, such as *-van-.* The vocabulary words in this lesson all have one of these roots.

Root	Meaning	English Word
-bell-	war	belligerent
-cid-	to kill, to cut	genocide
-cis-		incisive
-vinc-	to conquer	evince
-van-		vanquish

Words

bellicose

belligerent

concise

evict

evince

fratricide

genocide

incisive

invincible

vanquish

Unlocking Meaning

Write the vocabulary word that fits each clue below. Then say the word and write a short definition. Compare your definition and pronunciation with those on the flash card at the back of the book.

1. This word is always used as an adjective. It might be used to describe a person who always wants to start a fight or an argument.

   _____

   _____

   _____

2. This word is a combination of two Latin roots. One of the roots comes from the Latin word *frater,* meaning "brother."

   _____

   _____

   _____

3. This adjective has a prefix that means "not." If a football team is this, it never loses.

   _____

   _____

   _____

4. This word is a synonym for eject and suggests that before you can throw someone out you have to defeat the person.

_____

_____

_____

5. According to this word, if you can say a lot with a few words, you "cut" straight to the important information.

_____

_____

_____

6. The Greek word _genos,_ meaning "race," can be seen in this word.

_____

_____

_____

7. This word is related to incision, but it usually refers to a sharp mind instead of a sharp knife.

_____

_____

_____

8. This word is always a verb. You would not be able to do this to someone who is invincible.

_____

_____

_____

9. This verb came into English through the Latin word _evincere,_ meaning "to win a point," or "to prove." Today it is a synonym for "show."

_____

_____

_____

10. This word is similar in meaning to the answer for number 1, but it can be used as a noun or an adjective and can refer to a country or a person.

_____

_____

_____

Applying Meaning

Decide which word in parentheses best completes the sentence. Then write the sentence, adding the missing word.

1. Before attempting to climb that steep mountain cliff, we must condition our bodies and _____ our fear. (evince; vanquish)

   _____

   _____

2. The sight of all those A's and B's on my report card _____ that my long hours in the library had finally paid off. (evinced; vanquished)

   _____

   _____

3. The brothers never liked each other very much, but lately their relationship had turned utterly _____. (fratricidal; genocidal)

   _____

   _____

4. The _____ actions of the South American dictator provoked the neighboring countries to put their armies on alert. (bellicose; invincible)

   _____

   _____

5. The reporter provided a _____ summary of the city council meeting. (bellicose; concise)

   _____

   _____

Follow the directions below to write a sentence using a vocabulary word.

6. Describe someone you think is very intelligent and often sees the answer to a problem long before anyone else does. Use the word *incisive*.

   _____

   _____

   _____

7. Write a sentence about a historical event or period. Use the word *genocide*.

   _____

   _____

   _____

8. Use *evict* in a sentence about a cruel landlord.

_____

_____

_____

9. Complete the sentence: "Fareed showed his *belligerence* when he

_____."

_____

_____

_____

10. Describe a recent performance by your favorite sports team. Use the word *invincible*.

_____

_____

_____

Bonus Word

kowtow

In ancient China, people showed their deep respect for and obedience to the emperor by kneeling and touching, or knocking, the ground with their head. The Mandarin Chinese word for head was *tou*. The word for knock was *kou*. These words entered the English language as *kowtow*, meaning "to show respect or submission to another." The word is sometimes used in a negative way. Politicians might be accused of kowtowing to some special-interest group.

Write a Paragraph: Do you think people today still kowtow? For example, do they kowtow to television stars or movie stars? Choose something or someone to whom you feel people kowtow, and write a paragraph explaining why you feel that way.

Name _____

How well do you remember the words you studied in Lessons 1 through 3?
Take the following test covering the words from the last three lessons.

Part 1 Antonyms

Each question below includes a word in capital letters, followed by four
words or phrases. Choose the word or phrase that is most nearly <u>opposite</u>
in meaning to the word in capital letters. Consider all choices before deciding on your answer. Write the letter for your answer on the line provided.

Sample

S. GOOD	(A) simple	(B) bad	**S.** ___**B**___
	(C) able	(D) fast	

1. GLIB	(A) famous	(B) thoughtful	**1.** _____
	(C) dull	(D) ugly	
2. EVICT	(A) welcome	(B) eject	**2.** _____
	(C) resist	(D) acknowledge	
3. ELOQUENT	(A) silent	(B) ineffective	**3.** _____
	(C) ugly	(D) fancy	
4. INDIFFERENT	(A) strange	(B) concerned	**4.** _____
	(C) same	(D) careless	
5. CONCISE	(A) wordy	(B) concentrated	**5.** _____
	(C) clever	(D) convincing	
6. INVINCIBLE	(A) unconquered	(B) obvious	**6.** _____
	(C) transparent	(D) defeated	
7. GARRULOUS	(A) dangerous	(B) talkative	**7.** _____
	(C) quiet	(D) bright and colorful	
8. TRITE	(A) commonplace	(B) famous	**8.** _____
	(C) important	(D) stuffy	
9. HISTRIONIC	(A) sincere	(B) historic	**9.** _____
	(C) cheerful	(D) forgettable	
10. EVINCE	(A) cause	(B) combine	**10.** _____
	(C) recall	(D) hide	

Go on to next page. ➤

11. FEROCITY   (A) savagery   (B) kindness   11. _____
    (C) generosity   (D) metallic

12. ANGUISH   (A) poverty   (B) calm   12. _____
    (C) delight   (D) straight

13. BELLIGERENT   (A) peaceful   (B) noisy   13. _____
    (C) threatening   (D) patient

14. SUCCINCT   (A) wasteful   (B) vague   14. _____
    (C) failure   (D) comfortable

15. EFFUSIVE   (A) emotional   (B) sealed   15. _____
    (C) wasteful   (D) calm

Part 2 Matching Words and Meanings

Match the definition in Column B with the word in Column A.
Write the letter of the correct definition on the line provided.

Column A   **Column B**

16. incisive   a. a slow, difficult journey   16. _____

17. verbosity   b. a trick   17. _____

18. annihilation   c. a false show of courage   18. _____

19. ruse   d. total destruction   19. _____

20. bravado   e. wordiness   20. _____

21. harangue   f. an appeal or request   21. _____

22. petition   g. sharp and keen   22. _____

23. laconic   h. the murder of an entire people, race, or   23. _____
                           cultural group

24. genocide   i. brief and to the point   24. _____

25. trek   j. a long, loud speech   25. _____

Name _____

Lincoln Begins His Second Term

Historians have called the Civil War the defining moment in American history, a time when the issue of whether the states could be truly united would ultimately be answered. More than anyone else, Abraham Lincoln is credited with holding the union of states together.

5   Even though many people now consider Lincoln our greatest president, he was often scorned and ridiculed while he was in office. In fact, just a few short months before the voters cast their ballots in 1864, many felt Lincoln had little chance of winning reelection. People had grown tired of the war, and President Lincoln's popularity was at an all-time low. But
10 Lincoln did win reelection, and on March 4, 1865, the citizens of Washington gathered at the Capitol to witness his second oath of office. The scene has been recorded in numerous diaries and newspaper accounts.

All was quiet. Lincoln was about to **emerge** from the crowd, mount the podium, and raise his right hand to take his second oath of office. The
15 weather was dark and gloomy. Lincoln's tall, **gaunt** appearance seemed in perfect keeping with the dismal gray of the sunless sky. When the assembled crowd saw their president, the **solemnity** of the occasion gave way to applause. It rose to a powerful roar, then just as quickly **subsided.** At that exact moment the sun broke through the gray clouds that had
20 **shrouded** the scene since early morning, and shafts of sunlight shone on the speaker's platform. Many who witnessed the scene and recorded it in their diary saw this as an **omen** of good things to come in Lincoln's second term.

Lincoln had been forced to accept war rather than let the nation
25 **perish.** But now the outcome of the bloodiest conflict in American history seemed clear, and unlike those who sought to punish the South, Lincoln deeply desired that the nation become one again. He moved to the center of the platform and unfolded a single sheet of paper. As he began to speak, it was clear to everyone that his mind was now on peace,
30 not war.

With **malice** toward none; with **charity** for all; with firmness in the right, as God gives us to see the right, let us strive on to finish the work we are in; to bind up the nation's wounds; to care for him who shall have borne the battle, and for his widow, and his
35 orphan—to do all which may achieve and **cherish** a just and last- ing peace, among ourselves and with all nations.

With that, Lincoln ended the shortest swearing-in speech since George Washington's inauguration.

Words
charity
cherish
emerge
gaunt
malice
omen
perish
shroud
solemnity
subside

Unlocking Meaning

The sentences below are taken from the reading selection. Decide which word or words would best replace the vocabulary word in italic type. Write the letter for that word on the answer line.

1. Lincoln was about to *emerge* from the crowd, mount the podium, and raise his right hand to take his second oath of office.

    (A) escape   (B) turn away

    (C) hide   (D) come forth

    1. _____

2. Lincoln's tall, *gaunt* appearance seemed in perfect keeping with the dismal gray of the sunless sky.

    (A) lean   (B) foolish

    (C) humorous   (D) angry

    2. _____

3. When the assembled crowd saw their president, the *solemnity* of the occasion gave way to applause.

    (A) boredom   (B) confusion

    (C) ridiculousness   (D) seriousness

    3. _____

4. It [the applause] rose to a powerful roar, then just as quickly *subsided*.

    (A) changed   (B) turned away

    (C) declined   (D) became louder

    4. _____

5. At that exact moment the sun broke through the gray clouds that had *shrouded* the scene since early morning, and shafts of sunlight shone on the speaker's platform.

    (A) framed   (B) illuminated

    (C) hidden   (D) buried

    5. _____

6. Many who witnessed the scene and recorded it in their diary saw this as an *omen* of good things to come in Lincoln's second term.

    (A) example   (B) beginning

    (C) prediction   (D) representation

    6. _____

7. Lincoln had been forced to accept war rather than let the nation *perish*.

    (A) die   (B) grow old

    (C) prosper   (D) disappear

    7. _____

8. With *malice* toward none; with charity for all. . .

    (A) indifference   (B) kindness

    (C) suspicion   (D) ill will

    8. _____

9. With malice toward none; with *charity* for all. . .

    (A) indifference   (B) kindness

    (C) suspicion   (D) ill will

    9. _____

10. . . . to do all which may achieve and *cherish* a just and lasting peace, among ourselves and with all nations.

    (A) treasure   (B) ignore

    (C) avoid   (D) steal

    10. _____

Applying Meaning

Write the vocabulary word or a form of the vocabulary word that fits each clue below. Then use the word in a sentence.

1. Two synonyms are "kindness" and "generosity."

   _____

   _____

2. Breaking a mirror is considered a bad one. Finding a four-leaf clover is considered a good one.

   _____

   _____

3. Someone who has been ill or hungry might look this way.

   _____

   _____

4. Clothes for a dead person, or anything that hides or wraps something.

   _____

   _____

5. To love, to hold dear, to value highly.

   _____

   _____

6. Flood waters and thunderstorms will eventually do this.

   _____

   _____

7. Woodchucks do this from their burrows, and facts do this at a trial.

   _____

   _____

Write each sentence below. In the space write a form of the word in parentheses.

8. If Ted said that I cheated on the examination, he told a _____ lie. (malice)

_____

_____

_____

9. After she was nearly struck by the truck, Sue made a _____ vow never to cross before the light turns green. (solemnity)

_____

_____

_____

10. After the electricity failed, all the _____ food in the refrigerator spoiled. (perish)

_____

_____

_____

Mastering Meaning

Reread Lincoln's short speech on page 15. This speech was given in 1865, when the Civil War was coming to an end. Write a paragraph explaining how you think Lincoln planned to treat the people of the defeated Confederacy. Use some of the words we studied in this lesson.

Name _____

Some real and fictional people and places are so memorable for their characteristics that their name has come to have new meaning. Sometimes the name has so thoroughly taken on this new meaning that it is no longer capitalized, and few people remember that the word once was a name. All the words in this lesson came from proper nouns, but their current meaning has nothing to do with a name anymore.

Unlocking Meaning

Read the brief descriptions of the people and places below. Then choose the word or phrase that correctly completes the sentence. Write the letter for your choice on the answer line.

Words
bedlam
boycott
herculean
maudlin
maverick
mentor
mesmerize
nemesis
procrustean
quixotic

Charles C. Boycott was an English land agent in Ireland in the 1800s. When he refused to lower his rents, people decided to have nothing to do with him. Nowadays, if you *boycott* certain countries or businesses, you _____.

1. (A) accept them without reservation
   (B) refuse to deal with them
   (C) praise them openly
   (D) ask for a favor

The Hospital of Saint Mary of Bethlehem was an institution for the mentally ill in London. It was a noisy, confusing place. The name of the hospital was commonly shortened to Bedlam. Now *bedlam* has come to mean _____.

2. (A) medicine
   (B) a noisy, confusing place
   (C) religious devotion
   (D) a suburb of London

According to the Bible, Mary Magdalene was a reformed sinner. Artists often pictured her crying uncontrollably for her sins. From her name we get the word *maudlin*, which means _____.

3. (A) a Biblical scholar
   (B) highly religious
   (C) a fool
   (D) tearful and sentimental

According to Greek mythology, the goddess Nemesis avenged all injustices. Her justice was swift and certain. Today, when people meet their *nemesis,* they encounter _____.

4. (A) a beautiful goddess
   (B) a Greek storyteller
   (C) a foe who cannot be beaten
   (D) a heroic fictional character

1. _____

2. _____

3. _____

4. _____

Don Quixote, a character in a novel by Miguel de Cervantes, saw himself as a romantic knight. But he frequently rescued women who did not need rescuing and mistook windmills for evil giants. So when we call someone *quixotic,* we mean he or she is _____.

5. (A) sincere, but foolish

   (B) a modern warrior

   (C) the main character in a story

   (D) a person with poor eyesight

5. _____

Franz Mesmer was an 18th-century doctor who used hypnotic techniques to cause sleep-like reactions in his patients. Before long, the term *mesmerize* came to mean _____.

6. (A) to entertain

   (B) to hold spellbound

   (C) to create imaginary people and places

   (D) to prescribe unusual medicine

6. _____

Samuel Maverick was a rancher, but unlike other ranchers, he never branded his cattle. So naturally, when ranchers saw unbranded cattle roaming the range, they called them "mavericks." Today, a *maverick* is also _____.

7. (A) a person who does not follow the rules

   (B) a gambler

   (C) someone who loses his belongings

   (D) an unfenced area

7. _____

Hercules is a character from Greek mythology who gained immortality by performing twelve tasks requiring remarkable strength. Now, when a task is called *herculean,* it is thought to be _____.

8. (A) fascinating

   (B) immortal

   (C) imported from Greece

   (D) unusually difficult

8. _____

According to a popular Greek story, Procrustes invited people to lie in his bed. If they were too short for the bed, he stretched them to fit the bed. If they were too tall for the bed, he cut off their feet. Now someone who is *procrustean* will _____.

9. (A) ignore differences between individuals

   (B) protect innocent people

   (C) sleep on the floor

   (D) respect someone's personal needs

9. _____

Mentor was a trusted friend of the mythical Greek hero Odysseus. He was also the teacher of Odysseus's son and the manager of the house when Odysseus was gone. If a person is called your *mentor,* he or she is _____.

10. (A) a great hero

    (B) a trusted friend or advisor

    (C) someone who loves children

    (D) an identical twin

10. _____

Applying Meaning

Each question below contains at least one vocabulary word from this lesson. Answer each question "yes" or "no" in the space provided.

1. Would a business welcome a *boycott* by the residents of the neighborhood?

2. Would you be likely to find a *mentor* at a school or college?

3. When you study for an exam, do you try to *mesmerize* certain facts?

4. Does running a marathon after school require a *herculean* effort?

5. Would a *maudlin* person shed tears while watching a sad movie?

6. Would a *procrustean* individual usually agree with a *maverick*?

7. Would you expect to find the library in a state of *bedlam*?

8. If someone called your pledge to win an Olympic gold medal a *quixotic* dream, would you be flattered?

1. _____

2. _____

3. _____

4. _____

5. _____

6. _____

7. _____

8. _____

For each question you answered "no," write a sentence using the vocabulary word(s) correctly.

_____

_____

_____

_____

_____

_____

_____

_____

Write a sentence following the directions below.

9. Describe how a sports fan might look as he watches his favorite sport on television. Use a form of the word *mesmerize*.

_____

_____

_____

10. Describe something that you did that required great effort on your part. Use the word *herculean*.

_____

_____

_____

11. Describe a club with very strict rules for its members. Use the word *procrustean*.

_____

_____

_____

12. Describe the behavior of a real or imaginary person. Use the word *maverick*.

_____

_____

_____

Cultural Literacy Note

Pied Piper

According to an old German legend, the town of Hamelin was beset by a plague of rats. One day a man with a musical pipe and dressed in colorful, or "pied," clothing offered to get rid of the rats if the people of the town would pay for the service. The townspeople agreed, so the pied piper played his pipe and the rats followed him to the river and drowned.

When the piper demanded his payment, however, the townspeople refused to pay his fee. When they ignored his warnings, the pied piper began to play his pipe again. This time the children of the town followed him. The pied piper and all the children disappeared into a mountain and were never seen again. As a result of this popular story, a pied piper is thought to be anyone who entices or leads others, often through deceit or delusion.

Write a Paragraph: Are there modern-day pied pipers of our children and young people? Are certain types of music or television kinds of pied pipers? Choose your candidate for the modern pied piper. Explain your choice in a paragraph.

The Roots -doc-, -dox-, *and* -gno-

Name _____

The Latin word *docere* means "to teach." This word is the source of many English words and often appears as *-doc-* or *-doct-*. You sometimes see *-gno-* and *-dox-* in English words. They are parts of early Greek words and are combined with other affixes or word parts to form English words. The *-gno-* word part, which may appear as *-gnos-* or *-gni-,* means "know." The *-dox-* word part means "belief" or "opinion." All the words in this lesson contain one of these roots or word parts.

Root	Meaning	English Word
-doc-	to teach	doctrine
-dox-	belief, opinion	orthodox
-gno-	know	diagnose
-gni-		incognito

Unlocking Meaning

A vocabulary word appears in italics in each sentence or short passage below. Find the root or word part in the vocabulary word and think about how the word is used in the passage. Then write a definition for the vocabulary word. Compare your definition with the definition on the flash card.

1. Before she boarded the plane, the undercover police officer put on an elaborate disguise. It was important that she travel *incognito.*

_____

_____

_____

2. The candidate found he could not accept his party's *doctrine* on budgets and taxes, so he resigned his office.

_____

_____

_____

3. Before he could *diagnose* the problem with my car's engine, the mechanic had to check the gas tank and look for oil leaks.

_____

_____

_____

4. It seemed a great *paradox* to us, but the protesters claimed that after they were jailed they finally felt truly free. They saw no contradiction in saying this.

_____

_____

_____

Words

agnostic

cognomen

diagnose

docile

doctrinaire

doctrine

incognito

indoctrinate

orthodox

paradox

5. On the bus to the museum, the students were talkative and hard to control, but once we arrived, they became quite *docile*. They followed the guide's instructions and quietly filed into the lobby.

_____

_____

_____

6. Because one of his soldiers said he stood like a "stone wall" when the Union forces attacked, General Jackson's *cognomen* throughout the Civil War was "Stonewall."

_____

_____

_____

7. All of the religious arguments only confused Jamal more. He was not sure anyone knew for certain whether God existed. In the end, he announced that he would continue to be an *agnostic*.

_____

_____

_____

8. Maggie would listen to no one. Her *doctrinaire* attitude simply would not allow her to ask for help. To her, seeking help was a sign of weakness.

_____

_____

_____

9. My grandfather's beliefs on dating are quite *orthodox*. He says that the girl should never ask the boy for a date, and young people should never go out without an adult chaperon.

_____

_____

_____

10. Some parents feared the television program would *indoctrinate* the children against the values being taught at home and school. After all, the children are too young to know that everything they hear is not necessarily true.

_____

_____

_____

Applying Meaning

Read each sentence or short passage below. Write "correct" on the answer
line if the vocabulary word has been used correctly. Write "incorrect" on
the answer line if the vocabulary word has been used incorrectly.

1. Renata's *docile* personality caused her to challenge every request the
    teacher made. In the end, everyone simply ignored her.

    1. _____

2. Modern science often presents us with a *paradox*. Passenger planes
    can travel faster than the speed of sound, but we still have to wait for
    our luggage.

    2. _____

3. After weeks of worrying about what was going to happen, Juan
    decided to consult an *agnostic*.

    3. _____

4. New employees were given a short *indoctrination* to the company.
    They learned about its history, policies, and goals.

    4. _____

5. His company was founded on the simple but important *doctrine* that
    the customer must come first.

    5. _____

6. After years of hard work and study, my sister was awarded her
    doctrinaire from Columbia University. She plans to continue her
    studies in Europe.

    6. _____

7. His approach to art was quite *orthodox*. He studied the traditional
    masters, attended the accepted schools, and followed the standard
    examples.

    7. _____

8. The issues were complicated and difficult. Only a *cognomen* of
    experts could possibly arrive at a solution.

    8. _____

9. When it came to cooking, Avi was completely *incognito*. He hardly
    knew how to turn on a stove.

    9. _____

10. The doctor insisted on running a number of tests on the patient
    before attempting to *diagnose* the problem.

    10. _____

For each word used incorrectly, write a sentence using the word properly.

_____

_____

_____

_____

_____

_____

_____

_____

_____

_____

_____

_____

_____

_____

_____

_____

Our Living Language

When a new edition of a dictionary is published, it contains thousands of words that have recently been added to the language. Here are three terms that were recently added to the revised edition of one dictionary.

videophile   **sound bite**   **passive smoking**

Cooperative Learning: With a partner, write a definition for each of these words. Then make a list of three words you think might be added to the dictionary in the next few years, and write a definition of each.

Lessons 4–6

Name _____

How well do you remember the words you studied in Lessons 4 through 6? Take the following test covering the words from the last three lessons.

Part 1 Complete the Sentence

Decide which definition best completes the sentence. Write the letter for your choice on the answer line.

1. If you see an *omen,* you _____.
   (A) get a sign that something is going to happen
   (B) are watching an evil ritual
   (C) are bewitched
   (D) are reading the last words of a prayer

   1. _____

2. A *malicious* smile suggests a _____ attitude.
   (A) charming
   (B) tasteful
   (C) mean
   (D) casual

   2. _____

3. Someone with a *gaunt* appearance would be _____.
   (A) short, but husky
   (B) thin and bony
   (C) angry
   (D) serious

   3. _____

4. If you meet your *nemesis,* you run into someone you _____.
   (A) do not remember
   (B) dislike
   (C) cannot defeat
   (D) enjoy being with

   4. _____

5. If a group of people *boycott* a meeting, they _____.
   (A) refuse to attend
   (B) take it over
   (C) disrupt it
   (D) exclude women

   5. _____

6. A *maudlin* person might often be seen _____.
   (A) sleeping peacefully
   (B) looking for a fight
   (C) praying
   (D) crying

   6. _____

7. A club with *procrustean* rules for membership would _____.
   (A) be very expensive
   (B) ignore individual differences
   (C) be popular with the wealthy
   (D) probably be illegal

   7. _____

8. A *docile* pet would be _____.
   (A) kept away from children
   (B) easily managed
   (C) hard to control
   (D) large and muscular

   8. _____

9. If a famous athlete wants to be *incognito* in public, she desires _____.
   (A) her identity to be unknown
   (B) a great deal of attention
   (C) to be ignored
   (D) to be warm and friendly to her admirers

   9. _____

Go on to next page. ➤

10. If someone states a *paradox*, he _____.

    (A) says something with two   (B) is probably a mathematician
        meanings

    (C) is guilty of deceit   (D) is making a contradictory
                              statement that seems true

10. _____

11. When a storm *subsides*, it _____.

    (A) moves rapidly away   (B) breaks into parts

    (C) becomes less active   (D) increases in violence

11. _____

12. A *cherished* memory will _____.

    (A) never be forgotten   (B) be held dear

    (C) be the source of grief   (D) be kept secret

12. _____

13. Your *mentor* would be _____.

    (A) a trusted advisor   (B) an unconquered enemy

    (C) a secret admirer   (D) a rival or competitor

13. _____

14. If you found yourself *mesmerized* by something, you would be

    _____.

    (A) confused   (B) fascinated

    (C) annoyed   (D) fooled

14. _____

15. An *agnostic* is one who _____.

    (A) devotes himself to serving   (B) lives a life of strict discipline
        others

    (C) is knowledgeable about   (D) believes we can never know if
        agriculture   God exists

15. _____

Part 2 Matching Words and Meanings

Match the definition in Column B with the word in Column A.
Write the letter of the correct definition on the line provided.

Column A   **Column B**

16. charity   a. wrapping for a dead person or anything   **16.** _____
                     that conceals

17. perish   b. requiring great strength   **17.** _____

18. bedlam   c. to die or be destroyed   **18.** _____

19. diagnose   d. an independent thinker; nonconformist   **19.** _____

20. indoctrinate   e. noisy confusion   **20.** _____

21. quixotic   f. staying faithful to established beliefs   **21.** _____

22. maverick   g. kindness and love in judging others   **22.** _____

23. shroud   h. idealistic but foolish   **23.** _____

24. orthodox   i. to identify a disease or a condition   **24.** _____

25. herculean   j. to teach a certain set of principles   **25.** _____

Name _____

Earthquake

The shaking came at dawn, a sudden force they had no chance to escape. The young mother held her children close, trying to protect them. The father covered both his wife and children with his body, hoping to save them from falling limestone blocks. Their efforts were not
5   enough. Even though the **duration** of the earthquake was short, probably no more than a few minutes, the powerful forces were too much for the walls of the home. The family died, huddled together in their stone house. Along with hundreds of others that day, they were victims of an **immense** earthquake that struck southwest Cyprus in the year 365 A.D.

10   For thousands, perhaps millions of years, earthquakes have shaken our planet, causing the fearful destruction and **desolation** that the residents of Cyprus experienced on that fateful day. What conditions produce these powerful events? Can we predict where or when they will occur?

To understand something about earthquakes, you need to understand the
15   **structure** of our planet. The earth's crust is actually broken into huge plates. The continents ride on these plates, which **creep** over the earth's molten core. In some areas the edges of the plates **converge** and grind together, creating one type of earthquake. In other areas one plate may slip beneath another in a process called subduction. In some cases the
20   plates **diverge,** stretching and thinning the crust. This allows molten rock in the earth's core to rise. As this upwelling of extremely hot molten rock occurs, volcanos are created. Some long cracks, or faults, in the earth's surface are visible evidence of where two plates meet. If the plates are moving in different directions, earthquakes will persist in the **vicinity.**

25   Many severe earthquakes have occurred during recorded history, but it was not until the great San Francisco earthquake of 1906 that scientists began to study them. In trying to guess how the earth had moved, scientists built **theoretical** models to show the forces that had been involved. The studies showed that horizontal movement along the San
30   Andreas Fault had caused the Pacific and North American plates to mesh so tightly that no movement had occurred at the fault. Instead the strain along the edge of the Pacific plate had created an S-shaped warp. As the pressure increased, the strain grew, finally **culminating** in the edge of one plate snapping. This caused the two plates to grind along
35   each other, creating a strong vibration that traveled through the earth.

Earthquakes have taught us that the earth is constantly in motion. By using the data collected over hundreds of years, geologists can measure the power of the vibrations and, with the help of computers, map areas of hazardous regions. Although predictions are still very inexact,
40   earthquakes are finally yielding to scientific investigation.

Words
converge
creep
culminate
desolate
diverge
duration
immense
structure
theoretical
vicinity

Each word in this lesson's word list appears in dark type in the selection you just read. Think about how the vocabulary word is used in the selection, then write the letter for the best answer to each question.

1. Which word or words could best replace *duration* in line 5?
   (A) length of time   (B) communication
   (C) strength   (D) decline

   1. _____

2. Which word could best replace *immense* in line 9?
   (A) enormous   (B) tiny
   (C) moderate   (D) historic

   2. _____

3. Which word could best replace *desolation* in line 11?
   (A) crime   (B) plague
   (C) devastation   (D) domination

   3. _____

4. Which word could best replace *structure* in line 15?
   (A) makeup   (B) warps
   (C) history   (D) substance

   4. _____

5. Which word or words could best replace *creep* in line 16?
   (A) move slowly   (B) slip
   (C) linger   (D) rise

   5. _____

6. Which word or words could best replace *converge* in line 17?
   (A) confine   (B) separate
   (C) come together (D) convert

   6. _____

7. Which word could best replace *diverge* in line 20?
   (A) devise   (B) separate
   (C) travel   (D) revolve

   7. _____

8. Which word could best replace *vicinity* in line 24?
   (A) circle   (B) area
   (C) distance   (D) land

   8. _____

9. Which word could best replace *theoretical* in line 28?
   (A) pointless   (B) reliable
   (C) actual   (D) imaginary

   9. _____

10. Which word could best replace *culminating* in line 33?
    (A) declining   (B) climaxing
    (C) sinking   (D) starting

    10. _____

Applying Meaning

Follow the directions below to write a sentence using a vocabulary word.

1. Describe a series of events in a sport or similar activity. Use any form of the word *culminate*.

_____

_____

2. Describe some geographical feature in your city or town or something you saw on a trip or read about. Use the word *immense*.

_____

_____

3. Write a sentence telling about a topic you studied in one of your classes. Use any form of the word *structure*.

_____

_____

4. Describe a scene from a movie, book, or an event you have seen. Use any form of the word *desolate*.

_____

_____

5. Describe the movement of a person, animal, or object using any form of the word *creep*.

_____

_____

Read each sentence below. Write "correct" on the answer line if the vocabulary word has been used correctly. Write "incorrect" on the answer line if the vocabulary word has been used incorrectly.

6. The gym was closed for the *duration* of the year because of water damage.

6. _____

7. Allen asked us to *converge* his regrets to our hostess that he would not be able to attend the party.

7. _____

8. Rob and I had *diverging* opinions about how to raise money for the project.

8. _____

9. The Sasaki family was disappointed to find that there was no *vicinity* at the popular resort.

9. _____

10. One hundred years ago, traveling to the moon in a spaceship was only a *theoretical* possibility.

10. _____

11. As she watched the children gather a dandelion bouquet, a soft smile *crept* across her face.

11. _____

12. The Lopez family *culminates* cabbage and tomatoes in its garden.

12. _____

13. For the science fair, the class built a model showing the *structure* of the atom.

13. _____

14. The cake was so *desolate* that we all decided to have a second piece.

14. _____

For each word used incorrectly, write a sentence using the word properly.

_____

_____

_____

_____

_____

_____

_____

_____

_____

_____

_____

_____

_____

Mastering Meaning

Imagine that you are a newspaper reporter in the year 365 A.D. Your assignment is to write a story about the earthquake that recently occurred on the island of Cyprus. Write two paragraphs describing the damage and casualties. Use some of the words you studied in this lesson.

Name _____

The English language has the marvelous ability to borrow words freely from other languages. If no word exists in English for a thought or concept, we simply take a word from another language. After a time the pronunciation of the borrowed word may change to match English pronunciations, but sometimes we even keep the foreign pronunciation. The words in this lesson are all taken from the French language because no English word expresses the idea as well.

Unlocking Meaning

Read the sentences or short passages below. Write the letter for the correct definition of the italicized vocabulary word.

It is very difficult to become a member of the Greenfield Golf Club, but since my older brother is a member, he was my *entrée* to membership.

1. (A) legal advisor
   (B) the means to enter
   (C) obstacle
   (D) admission fee

We were very excited when the plane took off. I pressed my nose to the window and watched the city disappear below. The flight attendants, however, were quite *blasé* about it all. I wondered if they even knew we had taken off.

2. (A) exhilarated and talkative
   (B) worn out from prolonged or difficult work
   (C) distressed and frightened
   (D) bored and uninterested

The craft fair turned out to be a *potpourri* of exhibits. There were holiday ornaments made from cotton balls, cutting boards in the shapes of farm · animals, and even a stained-glass wind chime.

3. (A) odd or random collection of things
   (B) elaborate and expensive artwork
   (C) items made from pottery
   (D) old and outdated items

Why must things be as quiet as a mouse or as sly as a fox? Why couldn't they be as quiet as a cemetery or as sly as a riverboat gambler? Why use a *cliché* when a fresh expression will work?

4. (A) animal
   (B) overused expression
   (C) clever figure of speech
   (D) literary classic

Words
blasé
cliché
clientele
entrée
entrepreneur
gauche
naive
nonchalant
potpourri
rendezvous

1. _____

2. _____

3. _____

4. _____

We were free to explore the museums, parks, and stores all afternoon, but it was important that we *rendezvous* in the parking lot at six o'clock to board the bus home.

5. (A) avoid danger

   (B) render or give a report

   (C) meet

   (D) ask for directions

5. _____

Since it was my first trip to New York, I was quite *naive*. I stared up at the tall buildings, failed to tip the waiters, and got lost on the subways.

6. (A) clever and resourceful

   (B) angry

   (C) excessively curious or nosy

   (D) simple or inexperienced

6. _____

The spectators in the gymnasium were applauding and cheering wildly, but the captain of the basketball team acted quite *nonchalant* as he yawned and accepted the trophy.

7. (A) cool and unconcerned

   (B) confused and uncertain

   (C) shy and modest

   (D) embarrassed

7. _____

For months after the restaurant opened the owner lost money, but after a while he built up a *clientele* and his business began to show a good profit.

8. (A) group of regular customers or clients

   (B) debt

   (C) staff of clerks and assistants

   (D) communications system

8. _____

Not only did many people arrive late for the piano concert, they whispered and giggled throughout the performance. Such *gauche* behavior is inexcusable.

9. (A) humorous

   (B) gloomy

   (C) crude and awkward

   (D) informal and friendly

9. _____

After years of working in the factory, Joe Franklin decided to become an *entrepreneur.* So he quit his job, bought a truck, and painted "Joe's Moving Service" on its side.

10. (A) laborer

   (B) one who organizes or runs a business

   (C) foolish or irresponsible person

   (D) one who is unable to make up his mind

10. _____

Applying Meaning

Each question below contains at least one vocabulary word from this lesson. Answer each question "yes" or "no" in the space provided.

1. Would you want a firefighter to be *nonchalant* when coming to your rescue in a burning building?

2. Is it possible to have a quiet *rendezvous* in a restaurant or library?

3. Are *clichés* hard to remember?

4. Does a successful *entrepreneur* usually have a faithful *clientele*?

5. Are people usually *blasé* when taking their first ride on a roller coaster?

6. Could good grades in high school be your *entrée* to college?

1. _____

2. _____

3. _____

4. _____

5. _____

6. _____

For each question you answered "no," write a sentence using the vocabulary word correctly.

_____

_____

_____

_____

_____

_____

_____

_____

_____

_____

_____

_____

_____

Match the description or definition in Column B with the word in
Column A. Write the letter of the correct answer on the answer line.

Column A	Column B	
7. entrepreneur	a. a person who starts a business	7. _____
8. gauche	b. hodgepodge	8. _____
9. naive	c. a child who writes a letter to Santa Claus	9. _____
10. potpourri	d. someone who eats with his fingers at a fancy restaurant	10. _____

Bonus Words

C'est la vie   fait accompli

The French expression *C'est la vie* means "That's life." Its equivalent in English would be something like "What can you do?" It is an expression often used when things go wrong, but you feel powerless to do anything about it.

The French *fait accompli* translates as "accomplished fact." If you sneak into the kitchen and eat the last dessert, there is no point arguing about who should have it because there is little anyone can do about it. It is a fait accompli.

Write a Personal Narrative: Have you ever presented someone with a fait accompli or felt like saying "C'est la vie"? Write a short personal narrative describing something that happened to you or to someone you know that illustrates one of these expressions. Use the expression somewhere in your narrative, and try to use one or more of the vocabulary words as well.

Name _____

In Latin the word *cor* means "heart." This root can be found in a wide variety of English words because the heart is associated with both our physical bodies and our feelings and emotions. It sometimes appears as *-card-* or *-cord-*. The Latin word *currere* means "to run." It, too, appears in a wide range of words because *run* can have so many meanings. It may be spelled *-cur-*, *-cor-*, or *-cour-* in English words.

Root	Meaning	English Word
-cor-	heart	cordial
-card-		cardiac
-cur-	run	incursion
-cour-		recourse

Unlocking Meaning

A vocabulary word appears in italics in each sentence or short passage below. Find the root in each vocabulary word and choose the letter for the correct definition. Write the letter for your choice on the answer line.

1. The manager was very busy, so my application got only a *cursory* look. But the manager promised to study it carefully later.
   - (A) thorough
   - (B) silent
   - (C) quick
   - (D) humorous

2. After long hours of argument and debate over the issues, union and management representatives reached an *accord*. We can expect the strike to end soon.
   - (A) destination
   - (B) impossible obstacle
   - (C) victory
   - (D) harmonious agreement

3. The police officer tried to get the protestors to stop interfering with traffic, but they refused. In the end the only *recourse* was to arrest them.
   - (A) source of help or aid
   - (B) foolish desire
   - (C) college training
   - (D) thought or idea

4. The proposal to build a toxic waste dump was a source of *discord* in the community. Some citizens wanted the jobs that would be created. Others feared that the dump would affect their health.
   - (A) affection
   - (B) rope
   - (C) angry disagreement
   - (D) economic activity

Words

- accord
- cardiac
- cordial
- cursive
- cursory
- discord
- discursive
- precursor
- recourse
- recurrent

1. _____

2. _____

3. _____

4. _____

5. The dark clouds and high winds were *precursors* of the coming tornado.

   (A) forerunners   (B) proof

   (C) cause for swearing   (D) enemies

5. _____

6. The class was being taught to use a *cursive* style of writing instead of printing each letter.

   (A) foreign   (B) clever

   (C) impossible   (D) having letters run together

6. _____

7. It is easy to take notes on Ms. Eisner's lectures because her presentation is always very focused and direct. Mr. Todd's lectures, on the other hand, are quite *discursive.* I never know what he will say next.

   (A) disgusting   (B) discouraging

   (C) wide-ranging; rambling   (D) ordinary

7. _____

8. Because of Olga's history of *cardiac* problems, the doctor advised her not to overexercise.

   (A) related to the heart   (B) financial

   (C) digestive   (D) family

8. _____

9. Josh missed his old neighborhood. Ever since his family moved, he had *recurrent* dreams about the school and the friends he left behind.

   (A) frightening   (B) happening repeatedly

   (C) water-related   (D) distracting

9. _____

10. Since we had been such good friends for many years, I was not surprised by her *cordial* welcome.

   (A) hostile   (B) insincere

   (C) awkward   (D) warm and friendly

10. _____

Applying Meaning

Read each sentence or short passage below. Write "correct" on the answer line if the vocabulary word has been used correctly. Write "incorrect" on the answer line if the vocabulary word has been used incorrectly.

1. The school offered an American history *recourse* for any student who had failed the previous semester.

   1. _____

2. The master of ceremonies gave a *cursory* introduction; she knew everyone was eager to hear the main speaker.

   2. _____

3. For weeks after the book disappeared, June had one *recurrent* thought: Where could I have put it?

   3. _____

4. His performance in the championship game earned him the *accord* of the spectators and the players.

   4. _____

5. The argument ruined the dinner completely. Everyone left feeling quite *discursive* with the entire evening.

   5. _____

6. The development of the microchip was the *precursor* of a revolution in computer technology.

   6. _____

7. According to this report, *cardiac* patients at City Point Hospital get excellent care.

   7. _____

8. When Andre became angry, his language turned vulgar and *cursive*.

   8. _____

9. The heat had spoiled the fruits and vegetables, so we had to *discord* them.

   9. _____

10. They offered us a cold drink and a comfortable place to sit. We had not expected such a *cordial* welcome from the team we had just defeated.

    10. _____

For each word used incorrectly, write a sentence using the word properly.

_____

_____

_____

_____

_____

_____

_____

_____

_____

_____

_____

_____

_____

_____

Test-Taking Strategies

Some colleges require entering students to take a test of standard English grammar and usage. This test is often used to place students in a freshman English course.

These tests usually ask you to look at four underlined parts of a sentence and decide if one of these parts contains an error. You then write the letter for the underlined part that contains the error. If there is no error, you write E.

Sample

> **S.** <u>Everybody</u> on the basketball team <u>must take</u> <u>care of</u> <u>their</u> own   **S.** _____ **D** _____
>   A   B   C   D
> uniform. <u>No Error</u>
>   E

Always read the entire sentence before deciding on your answer. Look at each choice carefully. If you think you have found the error, ask yourself how you would correct it. There will be no more than one error. Can you tell why D is the correct answer to the sample question?

Practice: Write the letter for the underlined part of the sentence with an error. If there is no error, write E.

1. The <u>teacher's</u> assistant <u>has given</u> the assignment to <u>Frank, Julie,</u>   1. _____
        A   B   C
   and <u>myself.</u> <u>No Error</u>
          D   E

2. <u>Sam and I</u> love <u>to go</u> to the mall, <u>to look</u> for sea shells, and   2. _____
      A   B   C
   <u>playing</u> our favorite CDs. <u>No Error</u>
      D   E

3. If <u>you</u> go to the <u>meeting, please</u> <u>give</u> the message to <u>Anne and her.</u>   3. _____
       A   B   C   D
   <u>No Error</u>
      E

Name _____

How well do you remember the words you studied in Lessons 7 through 9?
Take the following test covering the words from the last three lessons.

Part 1 Antonyms

Each question below includes a word in capital letters, followed by four
words or phrases. Choose the word or phrase that is most nearly <u>opposite</u>
in meaning to the word in capital letters. Consider all choices before deciding on your answer. Write the letter for your answer on the line provided.

Sample

S. GOOD	(A) simple	(B) bad	**S.**	**B**
	(C) able	(D) fast		

1. IMMENSE	(A) great	(B) unimportant	**1.** _____
	(C) angry	(D) tiny	
2. CURSORY	(A) leisurely	(B) thorough	**2.** _____
	(C) manual	(D) blessed	
3. NONCHALANT	(A) casual	(B) chalant	**3.** _____
	(C) concerned	(D) brave	
4. CONVERGE	(A) separate	(B) convert	**4.** _____
	(C) resist	(D) reverse	
5. THEORETICAL	(A) religious	(B) practical	**5.** _____
	(C) frequent	(D) immoral	
6. DISCORD	(A) agreement	(B) argument	**6.** _____
	(C) musical	(D) sensible	
7. CLICHÉ	(A) slander	(B) unique remark	**7.** _____
	(C) proverb	(D) wisdom	
8. CORDIAL	(A) friendly	(B) dazed	**8.** _____
	(C) hostile	(D) remarkable	
9. NAIVE	(A) intelligent	(B) nice	**9.** _____
	(C) simple	(D) experienced	
10. GAUCHE	(A) refined	(B) clumsy	**10.** _____
	(C) unusual	(D) familiar	

Go on to next page. ➤

11. DESOLATE   (A) solid   (B) prosperous   11. _____
                         (C) foreign   (D) convenient

12. CULMINATE   (A) initiate   (B) destroy   12. _____
                         (C) reward   (D) elevate

13. BLASÉ   (A) extinguished   (B) difficult   13. _____
                         (C) injured   (D) excited

14. POTPOURRI   (A) hodgepodge   (B) orderly   14. _____
                                               arrangement
                         (C) sober   (D) elaborate

15. DISCURSIVE   (A) direct   (B) repulsive   15. _____
                         (C) appealing   (D) handwritten

Part 2 Matching Words and Meanings

Match the definition in Column B with the word in Column A.
Write the letter of the correct definition on the line provided.

Column A	Column B	
16. vicinity	a. pertaining to the heart	16. _____
17. diverge	b. area or region	17. _____
18. entrepreneur	c. to meet at a certain time and place	18. _____
19. recurrent	d. one's group of customers	19. _____
20. rendezvous	e. to move in different directions	20. _____
21. cardiac	f. occurring again	21. _____
22. duration	g. method of entry	22. _____
23. precursor	h. length of time	23. _____
24. entrée	i. one who runs a business	24. _____
25. clientele	j. forerunner	25. _____

Name _____

"Laissez les bons temps rouler!" ("Let the good times roll!")

It's difficult to resist tapping toes, let alone dancing feet, when the hard-driving rhythms and **robust** tones of Cajun music throb and pound. **Indigenous** to the Louisiana bayous where it developed, this unique sound was nourished by the New World. Like jazz, rock, and the blues,
5   Cajun music is a unique **synthesis** of cultural elements. Its lyrics come from French folklore, while its wailing singing style can be traced to the chants of Native Americans. Spanish explorers contributed the guitar, German immigrants supplied the accordion, and African Americans reshaped the fiddle dance tunes with percussion techniques. Lively
10 and infectious, Cajun music **traverses** cultural, generational, and language barriers.

To the Cajuns, however, music is much more than entertainment; it is a link with their treasured but tragic history. The word *Cajun* is an alteration of the word *Acadian,* which refers to the seventeenth-century
15 French colonists who settled in Nova Scotia. Although the Acadians declared neutrality in the rivalry between France and England for **dominion** of North America, the British demanded loyalty when they claimed the area in 1715. In a mass deportation executed with cold **ruthlessness,** British soldiers collected thousands of French Canadians,
20 packed them into boats, and shipped them to widely dispersed areas.

Many of the exiled Acadians settled in remote southwestern Louisiana, where their isolation allowed them to evolve into a distinct, tight-knit ethnic group. When the oil development and road-building programs of World War I brought modern America rushing in, however, the Cajun
25 parishes could no longer resist **acculturation.** In the headlong attempt to become part of the larger society, the language and music were discouraged, **quelled,** and all but forgotten.

In the mid-1970s, many Americans became interested in searching for their roots. As part of this heritage movement, Cajun music was rescued
30 and **validated** as an important folk-music tradition. Today, it is one of the fastest growing regional sounds in the United States. In addition to being played in live concerts, in clubs, and on the radio, Cajun songs appear in movie scores, in the introductions for television situation comedies, and in commercials.

35 Having survived centuries of adversity, isolation, and persecution, the music tells **plaintive** stories about loneliness and lost love. Yet there is nothing depressing about this music. Set against what the Cajuns call a "chanky-chank" beat, the songs urge everyone to sing, dance, laugh, and "let the good times roll."

Words
acculturate
dominion
indigenous
plaintive
quell
robust
ruthless
synthesis
traverse
validate

Each word in this lesson's word list appears in dark type in the selection you just read. Think about how the vocabulary word is used in the selection, then write the letter for the best answer to each question.

1. Which word could best replace *robust* in line 2?
   (A) confusing   (B) strong
   (C) quiet   (D) childish

   1. _____

2. Which word could best replace *indigenous* in line 3?
   (A) native   (B) baffling
   (C) forgiving   (D) unknown

   2. _____

3. A *synthesis* (line 5) can best be described as a(n) _____.
   (A) denial   (B) lesson
   (C) opinion   (D) combination

   3. _____

4. Which word or words could best replace *traverses* in line 10?
   (A) passes across   (B) signals
   (C) imposes   (D) slows down

   4. _____

5. Which word could best replace *dominion* in line 17?
   (A) exploration   (B) unification
   (C) control   (D) delegation

   5. _____

6. *Ruthlessness* (line 19) can best be described as _____.
   (A) simplicity   (B) cruelty
   (C) sacrifice   (D) courage

   6. _____

7. *Acculturation* (line 25) is a process that involves _____.
   (A) monetary gain   (B) deportation
   (C) government influence (D) adaptation

   7. _____

8. Which word could best replace *quelled* in line 27?
   (A) resisted   (B) honored
   (C) suppressed   (D) tolerated

   8. _____

9. Which word or words could best replace *validated* in line 30?
   (A) confirmed   (B) exported
   (C) reacted to   (D) sickened

   9. _____

10. *Plaintive* (line 36) stories are _____.
    (A) joyous   (B) mournful
    (C) repetitious   (D) unrelated

    10. _____

Applying Meaning

Decide which word in parentheses best completes the sentence.
Then write the sentence, adding the missing word.

1. To report on the conclusions reached by the group, the leader _____ the opinions and ideas of all the members. (quelled; synthesized)

_____

_____

2. In order to prove or disprove hypotheses, scientists must _____ their test results. (acculturate; validate)

_____

_____

3. Hannibal is credited even today with one of the greatest troop move-ments in history because he led an army of 100,000 in _____ the Alps. (traversing; validating)

_____

_____

4. Sociologists, interested in the way groups or societies come together and influence one another, study how they _____. (acculturate; traverse)

_____

_____

5. Tantalus, a king in classical mythology, was punished _____ by the gods for offending them; every time he reached for a fruit-laden branch of the tree that was just above his head, the wind blew it out of his reach. (plaintively; ruthlessly)

_____

_____

Read each sentence or short passage below. Write "correct" on the answer line if the vocabulary word has been used correctly. Write "incorrect" on the answer line if the vocabulary word has been used incorrectly.

6. Homeless people in major cities are *indigenous.* They cannot afford to rent or buy homes.

6. _____

7. Even when perfectly content, the Siamese cat makes a *plaintive* cry that gives the impression that it is lonely and miserable.

7. _____

8. With the exception of a six-year period when it was under the *domin-ion* of Italy, Ethiopia has withstood European attempts at colonization.

8. _____

9. The *robust* tree had a reed-thin trunk that looked as if a light breeze would topple it.

9. _____

10. The owners of the factory *quelled* the effects of the strike by bringing in scabs, or strikebreakers, to maintain production.

10. _____

For each word used incorrectly, write a sentence using the word properly.

_____

_____

_____

_____

_____

_____

_____

_____

_____

_____

_____

_____

_____

_____

_____

_____

Mastering Meaning

Suppose that you are the music critic for your school newspaper. A new Cajun group has just released an album that you want to review. Use your imagination to create a name for the group and for some of its songs. Then write a music review that will introduce your readers to Cajun music and will let them know what they can expect to hear on this album. In your review, use some of the words we studied in this lesson.

Name _____

The process by which people govern themselves is both complex and curious. On the one hand it involves deep philosophical thought; on the other it is as practical as a campaign poster. Our language has spawned numerous words to describe this process and the personalities and philosophies involved in this arena of human experience. In this lesson you will learn ten words that stand for concepts of law and government.

Words
autonomy
bureaucracy
codify
despot
imperious
reactionary
sedition
sovereign
totalitarian
usurp

Unlocking Meaning

Read the sentences or short passages below. Write the letter for the correct definition of the italicized vocabulary word.

It was their fear of *sedition* that prompted the authorities to ban all opposition newspapers and radio stations. In addition, all suspected agitators were confined to jail indefinitely.

1. (A) unfair elections
    (B) conduct likely to incite rebellion
    (C) popular support
    (D) gossip and rumors

The once popular ruler began to ignore the well-being of the citizens, and since no one questioned his authority, he gradually turned into a *despot*.

2. (A) a fair and effective ruler
    (B) democratically elected officeholder
    (C) military officer
    (D) a tyrant with absolute authority

The residents of the island expelled the foreign ministers and proclaimed their *autonomy*. Never again would they bow to another country's flag.

3. (A) freedom and independence
    (B) desire for peace
    (C) dependence on the protection of another nation
    (D) connection with a political party

The president complained that the proposed law would *usurp* his authority as commander-in-chief of the military. The constitution clearly stated that only the president could order an attack.

4. (A) enlarge
    (B) illegally take away
    (C) confuse
    (D) drain or exhaust

1. _____

2. _____

3. _____

4. _____

The government plan to offer tuition assistance to deserving students in poor neighborhoods made sense. But by the time applications worked their way through the *bureaucracy,* many deserving students got tired of waiting and dropped out of the program.

5. (A) local elected officials
   (B) democratic process
   (C) inefficient system of offices and rules
   (D) postal system

5. _____

The proposed reforms in the welfare and health care system had little chance of passing. The expected *reactionary* attitudes began to surface among those quite happy with the way things were.

6. (A) opposed to change
   (B) soft-spoken
   (C) humorous
   (D) medical

6. _____

The candidate's *imperious* manner may have lost him the election. In a democracy, people have a right to expect elected officials to be their servants, and not the other way around.

7. (A) humble and soft spoken
   (B) arrogant and dictatorial
   (C) hard and resistant
   (D) appealing

7. _____

After decades of passing numerous laws and regulations, it was essential that the government attempt to *codify* its work. It had reached the point where judges had difficulty understanding what the law required.

8. (A) translate
   (B) repeal
   (C) arrange and systematize
   (D) legalize

8. _____

Before the United States could come into being, the individual states had to surrender some of their *sovereign* rights.

9. (A) having authority to govern
   (B) financial
   (C) unconstitutional
   (D) illegal

9. _____

After overthrowing the elected officials, the military commander installed a *totalitarian* government. From that time on, even the simplest action required his approval.

10. (A) reformed and improved
    (B) efficient and orderly
    (C) emphasizing personal concern for its citizens
    (D) exercising absolute control

10. _____

Applying Meaning

Decide which word in parentheses best completes the sentence. Then write the sentence, adding the missing word.

1. After the prime minister dissolved parliament, packed the court with his appointees, and cancelled elections, the United States declared it could no longer recognize such a _____ form of government. (bureaucratic; totalitarian)

   _____

   _____

2. By giving the president the right to revise the bill, the senators had allowed their authority to be _____. (codified; usurped)

   _____

   _____

3. The South refused to accept the authority of federal authorities, insisting that _____ lay with the individual states. (bureaucracy; sovereignty)

   _____

   _____

4. Her _____ attitude was predictable. She voted against every bill that would have reformed the election laws. (bureaucratic; reactionary)

   _____

   _____

5. The president declared he would not tolerate acts of terrorism, assassination, or any other _____ acts against the government. (despotic; seditious)

   _____

   _____

Each question below contains a vocabulary word from this lesson. Answer each question "yes" or "no" in the space provided.

6. Was the Revolutionary War fought to make the colonies *autonomous*?   6. _____

7. When the military authorities take over the government, would you expect them to *codify* the former officials?   7. _____

8. Would a despot be found in a *totalitarian* country?   8. _____

9. Should a candidate demonstrate an *imperious* attitude when
campaigning for votes?

9. _____

10. Does a ruler welcome the opportunity to have his authority *usurped?*

10. _____

For each question you answered "no," write a sentence using the vocabulary word correctly.

_____

_____

_____

_____

_____

_____

_____

_____

_____

_____

_____

Bonus Word

gerrymander

In 1812, Governor Gerry of Massachusetts and his political allies had the district lines redrawn in ways that gave his party an unfair advantage in future elections. One such district was shaped like a salamander, a long lizard-like animal. It was not long before the newspapers began referring to the senators elected from such districts as gerrymanders, a combination of *salamander* and *Gerry,* the governor whose party was responsible for these strangely shaped districts. In addition, the political strategy of drawing political districts so as to give one party an unfair advantage has been called gerrymandering ever since.

Write a Position Paper: Today, district lines are sometimes drawn to ensure that a minority group will be represented. Write a brief position paper outlining how you feel about such a practice. Use some vocabulary words you have studied.

Name _____

The Latin word *manus* means "hand." Elements of this Latin word appear in many modern English words. For example, work done with the hands is called manual labor. The Latin word *ped,* on the other hand, means foot. A pedestrian is someone traveling on foot. The Greek language had a slightly different word, *pod,* for foot, so it is not unusual to see this root in English words, especially scientific words. It is not always easy to see the "hands" and "feet" meanings in modern English words. For example, the hand is associated with giving, so in a word like *countermand,* the *-man-* root refers to giving an order.

Root	Meaning	English Word
-man-	hand	manipulate
-ped-	foot	expedite
-pod-		podium

Words

countermand

expedite

impediment

mandate

mandatory

manipulate

pedestal

pedigree

podiatrist

podium

Unlocking Meaning

A vocabulary word appears in italics in each sentence or short passage below. Find the root in each vocabulary word and choose the letter for the correct definition. Write the letter for your answer on the line provided.

1. Lying across the bicycle path, the tree was an *impediment*. We had no choice but to walk around it.
   (A) embarrassment   (B) obstacle
   (C) curiosity   (D) reminder

2. Our mayor has a fascinating *pedigree*. Her grandfather was the first state senator, and her great-grandfather was one of the state's earliest settlers.
   (A) list of ancestors   (B) imagination
   (C) type of political party (D) secret

   1. _____

3. In addition to studying the human anatomy, a surgeon must learn to *manipulate* complicated instruments and machines.
   (A) repair   (B) control with the hands
   (C) explain in detail   (D) move or position

   2. _____

   3. _____

4. The lieutenant's decision to attack meant certain disaster. Fortunately, the captain was able to *countermand* the order and save the regiment.
   (A) understand   (B) analyze and compare
   (C) reverse   (D) write out

   4. _____

5. In order to *expedite* the shipment, the mechanic phoned in the order and asked the supplier to send the parts on the next plane.

    (A) check carefully   (B) cancel

    (C) delay   (D) speed up

5. _____

6. The lecturer stepped to the *podium,* looked straight at the audience, and slowly began to read from his notes.

    (A) stand for holding notes   (B) type of speaker

    (C) curtain   (D) someone who introduces
                                  a speaker

6. _____

7. Before anyone can purchase a handgun, there is a *mandatory* five-day waiting period while a background check of the purchaser is conducted.

    (A) for men only   (B) required

    (C) prolonged   (D) illegal

7. _____

8. After the basketball star began seeing the *podiatrist* regularly, the pain began to disappear and his game improved considerably.

    (A) foot doctor   (B) type of physical therapist

    (C) fortune teller   (D) sports psychologist

8. _____

9. The candidate's huge victory in the election was interpreted as a *mandate* for all the new programs she proposed during the campaign.

    (A) rejection   (B) symbol

    (C) fascination   (D) authorization

9. _____

10. The statue was lowered carefully onto the *pedestal.* From this prominent new position, it would now be the main attraction of the museum.

    (A) foundation   (B) balcony

    (C) outdoor arena   (D) pedestrian walkway

10. _____

Applying Meaning

Decide which word in parentheses best completes the sentence. Then write
the sentence, adding the missing word.

1. The project was seriously behind schedule, so the manager hired a
    construction specialist to recommend ways to _____ the work.
    (expedite; impede)

    _____

    _____

    _____

2. Due to a clerical error, the package was dispatched to the wrong loca-
    tion. Before anyone could _____ the order, the contents had
    spoiled. (countermand; mandate)

    _____

    _____

    _____

3. Because the coach was on the league committee, he was able to
    _____ the schedule so his team played only the weaker
    teams. (mandate; manipulate)

    _____

    _____

    _____

4. The Heritage Women's Club was so exclusive, anyone wishing to join
    had to trace her _____ back to the Revolutionary War.
    (pedestal; pedigree)

    _____

    _____

    _____

5. The blisters became so infected and painful that I finally had to
    consult a _____. (podiatrist; podium)

    _____

    _____

    _____

Read each sentence or short passage below. Write "correct" on the answer line if the vocabulary word has been used correctly. Write "incorrect" on the answer line if the vocabulary word has been used incorrectly.

6. The chemist carefully measured the *podium* before placing it in the solution. Even a slight miscalculation would ruin the experiment.

6. _____

7. In order to be considered for the job, all applicants had to pass a *mandatory* drug test.

7. _____

8. Hawaii's crops include pineapple, avocados, and *mandates*.

8. _____

9. The hikers soon realized they should not have packed so much canned food. The extra weight was a serious *impediment* to their progress.

9. _____

10. The shipment of shoes was stored in a *pedestal* inside the warehouse until the store could be remodeled.

10. _____

For each word used incorrectly, write a sentence using the word properly.

_____

_____

_____

_____

_____

_____

_____

_____

Our Living Language

pedigree

In medieval times, wealth and power often depended on one's ancestry. Great care was taken in charting the family tree. These charts used lines resembling the footprint of a crane, a long-legged bird. In French, these were called *pied de grue*, meaning "foot of a crane." The term came to refer to the chart itself. It entered the English language around 1500 and eventually became *pedigree*, meaning ancestry or the chart of one's family tree.

Use an Unabridged Dictionary: Find the history of these words:

peddle   manacle   maneuver   manuscript

Name _____

How well do you remember the words you studied in Lessons 10 through 12? Take the following test covering the words from the last three lessons.

Part 1 Choose the Correct Meaning

Each question below includes a word in capital letters, followed by four words or phrases. Choose the word or phrase that is <u>closest</u> in meaning to the word in capital letters. Write the letter for your answer on the line provided.

Sample

S. FINISH	(A) enjoy	(B) complete	**S.** ____**B**____
	(C) destroy	(D) enlarge	

1. INDIGENOUS	(A) native	(B) careful	**1.** _____
	(C) poor	(D) industrious	
2. SYNTHESIS	(A) illegal act	(B) combination	**2.** _____
	(C) artificial	(D) systematic	
3. DESPOT	(A) railroad station	(B) outlaw	**3.** _____
	(C) tyrant	(D) regulation	
4. MANDATE	(A) authorization	(B) amendment	**4.** _____
	(C) tropical fruit	(D) historic event	
5. USURP	(A) seize illegally	(B) inhale deeply	**5.** _____
	(C) attack	(D) consume	
6. IMPEDIMENT	(A) importance	(B) type of vehicle	**6.** _____
	(C) foundation	(D) obstacle	
7. AUTONOMY	(A) automatic	(B) independence	**7.** _____
	(C) royal decree	(D) dictatorship	
8. RUTHLESS	(A) ancient	(B) benevolent	**8.** _____
	(C) cruel	(D) plain and simple	
9. QUELL	(A) to quiet	(B) writing instrument	**9.** _____
	(C) to overthrow	(D) to confuse	
10. VALIDATE	(A) to value	(B) to prove correct	**10.** _____
	(C) to elect to office	(D) to assist	
11. SEDITION	(A) withdrawal	(B) drugged state	**11.** _____
	(C) negotiation	(D) rebellious behavior	
12. REACTIONARY	(A) very conservative	(B) counterattack	**12.** _____
	(C) progressive	(D) old-fashioned	

Go on to next page. ➤

13. PODIATRIST   (A) architect   (B) foot doctor   13. _____
                    (C) gloomy person   (D) fortune teller

14. ROBUST   (A) sensible   (B) weak   14. _____
                    (C) punctured   (D) vigorous

15. COUNTERMAND   (A) cancel   (B) government clerk   15. _____
                    (C) conceal   (D) official document

Part 2 Complete the Sentence

Decide which definition best completes the sentence. Write the letter for
your choice on the answer line.

16. If a department store promised to *expedite* your order, you would   16. _____
     expect it _____.
     (A) to be replaced   (B) to arrive quickly
     (C) to be damaged   (D) to be delayed

17. A school with a *mandatory* entrance examination would _____.   17. _____
     (A) be open to men only   (B) test physical coordination
     (C) require applicants to pass a test   (D) probably be very strict

18. A country with a *totalitarian* form of government would probably   18. _____
     _____.
     (A) hold regular elections   (B) regulate the press
     (C) enjoy popular support   (D) be run by religious leaders

19. When listening to a *plaintive* song, the audience might _____.   19. _____
     (A) cry   (B) laugh
     (C) suddenly stand up   (D) feel embarrassed

20. In which of these would you be most likely to encounter a *bureaucracy?*   20. _____
     (A) a small family   (B) a bedroom
     (C) the school playground   (D) a large government agency

21. A *sovereign* nation is one that _____.   21. _____
     (A) is free and independent   (B) has a king or queen
     (C) is occupied by a foreign power   (D) invades another nation

22. If a bookkeeper tries to *manipulate* the numbers in a company's   22. _____
     records, he or she is attempting to _____ them.
     (A) alter or change   (B) double check
     (C) destroy   (D) erase

23. If you *traverse* a soccer field, you _____ it.   23. _____
     (A) measure   (B) inspect
     (C) change   (D) walk across

24. If one country has *dominion* of another, it _____ it.   24. _____
     (A) borders on   (B) rules
     (C) has a low opinion of   (D) fears

25. Someone who brags about his or her *pedigree* might _____.   25. _____
     (A) claim to have met the president   (B) say his dog just won a
                                              blue ribbon
     (C) claim his grandfather was royalty   (D) be arrested

Name _____

"I Have a Dream"—Dr. Martin Luther King Jr.

Our Constitution guarantees certain civil rights to all citizens of the United States. However, not long ago these rights were often **abridged** by local or state laws. These laws created segregated schools and limited voting rights by requiring so-called literacy tests or imposing poll taxes
5   designed to keep African Americans from voting.

For decades, a number of civil rights groups fought these restrictions, but progress was painfully slow. It took the words and actions of Dr. Martin Luther King Jr. to renew and **galvanize** the movement.

This articulate and **charismatic** African American minister inspired an
10   entire generation that had grown impatient for change. Dr. King had for many years been an **indefatigable** worker for civil rights. His frequent, nonviolent efforts on behalf of equality often landed him in jail.

On August 28, 1963, King spoke to the more than 250,000 people assembled in the nation's capital and to millions of Americans on live television.
15   This remarkable speech gave the civil rights movement new strength.

> I say to you today, my friends, that in spite of the difficulties and **frustrations** of the moment, I still have a dream. It is a dream deeply rooted in the American dream.

> I have a dream that one day this nation will rise up and live out
20   the true meaning of its **creed:** "We hold these truths to be self-evident, that all men are created equal . . . ."

> I have a dream that my four little children will one day live in a nation where they will not be judged by the color of their skin, but by the content of their **character** . . . .

25   > So let freedom ring from the prodigious hilltops of New Hampshire . . . .

> Let freedom ring from the curvaceous peaks of California . . . .

> When we let freedom ring, when we let it ring from every village and every hamlet, from every state and every city, we will be able
30   to speed up that day when all of God's children — black men and white men, Jews and Gentiles, Protestants and Catholics — will be able to join hands and sing in the words of the old Negro spiritual, "Free at last! Free at last! Thank God Almighty, we are free at last!"

Delivered before the Lincoln Memorial, these words are among the most
35   **renowned** and often quoted in American history. They had an immediate and **immeasurable** impact upon the nation and upon the civil rights movement in the years that followed. A series of civil rights acts were **eventually** passed, and the long road to Dr. King's dream become a little shorter.

Words

- **abridge**
- **character**
- **charismatic**
- **creed**
- **eventual**
- **frustration**
- **galvanize**
- **immeasurable**
- **indefatigable**
- **renown**

Each word in this lesson's word list appears in dark type in the selection you just read. Think about how the vocabulary word is used in the selection, then write the letter for the best answer to each question.

1. Which word could best replace *abridged* in line 2?
   (A) expanded   (B) improved
   (C) limited   (D) transferred

   1. _____

2. Which word or words could best replace *galvanize* in line 8?
   (A) cut short   (B) reduce
   (C) exhaust   (D) energize

   2. _____

3. Which word could best replace *charismatic* in line 9?
   (A) boring   (B) simple
   (C) wealthy   (D) magnetic

   3. _____

4. Which word could best replace *indefatigable* in line 11?
   (A) sluggish   (B) tireless
   (C) defeated   (D) ineffective

   4. _____

5. Which word could best replace *frustrations* in line 17?
   (A) successes   (B) disappointments
   (C) ideas   (D) anger

   5. _____

6. A *creed* (line 20) is a(n) _____.
   (A) anthem   (B) arrangement
   (C) belief   (D) proud boast

   6. _____

7. *Character* (line 24) is a person's _____.
   (A) appearance   (B) ideas
   (C) religious beliefs (D) good and bad qualities

   7. _____

8. Which word could best replace *renowned* in line 35?
   (A) ignored   (B) ridiculed
   (C) famous   (D) unusual

   8. _____

9. Which word could best replace *immeasurable* in line 36?
   (A) enormous   (B) immediate
   (C) uncertain   (D) small

   9. _____

10. Which word could best replace *eventually* in line 37?
    (A) finally   (B) never
    (C) rudely   (D) foolishly

    10. _____

Name _____

Applying Meaning

Follow the directions below to write a sentence using a vocabulary word.

1. Describe an experience you have had in school, on a job, or at home. Use a form of the word *frustrate*.

    _____

    _____

    _____

2. Describe the effect of some historic event using any form of the word *immeasurable*.

    _____

    _____

    _____

3. Complete the following: The Peace Corps is looking for young men and women of good *character*. All applicants must . . . .

    _____

    _____

    _____

4. Use any form of the word *renown* to describe an athlete, movie star, or musical group.

    _____

    _____

    _____

5. Describe a real or imaginary person you feel has worked hard on behalf of an important cause such as the environment or a political candidate. Use a form of the word *indefatigable*.

    _____

    _____

    _____

Read each sentence or short passage below. Write "correct" on the answer line if the vocabulary word has been used correctly. Write "incorrect" on the answer line if the vocabulary word has been used incorrectly.

6. The mayor's demand that the newspaper stop publishing critical editorials was met with numerous protests. Most citizens felt this was an *abridgement* of the freedom of the press.

6. _____

7. The police investigation proved conclusively that the professor was really a *charisma*. He had fooled everyone into thinking he was a famous scientist.

7. _____

8. Until the accident, residents had shown little interest in the traffic problems. But seeing one of their neighbors lying injured on the street *galvanized* their efforts to reduce the speed limit.

8. _____

9. If we practice hard every day after school and follow the coach's directions, the *eventual* victory will be ours.

9. _____

10. The rusty hinges on the door made an eerie *creed* as it swung back and forth in the evening breeze.

10. _____

For each word used incorrectly, write a sentence using the word properly.

_____

_____

_____

_____

_____

_____

_____

_____

_____

Mastering Meaning

Martin Luther King's speech had a strong impact on his audience. In addition to his powerful use of words, he had a remarkable talent for stating things in memorable ways. In his August 1963 speech he repeated the phrase "I have a dream . . ." several times, building slowly to the climactic "Free at last!" Write a series of statements stating your dream for the future of our nation. Begin each statement with "I have a dream . . ." Use some words you studied in this lesson.

Name _____

You may not agree with the old saying, "Money makes the world go 'round," but it is hard to deny that money and business play an important part in everyone's life. It is no surprise then that our language has so many words to describe our interactions in the areas of money and business. In this lesson you will learn ten words frequently used in the world of business and money.

Unlocking Meaning

Read the sentences or short passages below. Write the letter for the correct definition of the italicized vocabulary word.

At the annual meeting of the nation's popcorn growers, the growers decided to form a *cartel* to set the prices charged by all the producers.

1. (A) an association of producers in a particular industry that works to improve the industry's image
    (B) an association of producers in a particular industry that buys out the smaller producers
    (C) an association of producers in a particular industry that works to control the market
    (D) an association of producers in a particular industry that works to influence public officials and legislators

An advantage of keeping your money in a savings account is that your money will *accrue* interest.

2. (A) invest
    (B) accumulate over time
    (C) discount
    (D) keep track of

The drug company printed long warnings on packages of its new drug in an attempt to *indemnify* itself from legal action in case the medicine had some unexpected side effects.

3. (A) insure or protect against loss, damage, or injury
    (B) safeguard the reputation of a person or business
    (C) use the media to inform the public about a product
    (D) cause a movement to gain strength or vigor

The United States was able to industrialize because it had workers and natural resources. Perhaps most important, it had the *capital* and the confidence to spend it building factories and railroads, knowing such investments would pay for themselves in the long run.

4. (A) the most important kind of wealth a person possesses
    (B) money loaned to a company by others
    (C) wealth that comes from land
    (D) wealth that is used to produce more wealth

Words

accrue

audit

capital

cartel

collateral

indemnify

liquidate

lucrative

pecuniary

usury

1. _____

2. _____

3. _____

4. _____

No one could understand how Inez Santos could leave a *lucrative* job on Wall Street to go back to art school. Inez said she didn't mind giving up a few luxuries for a more personal challenge.

5. (A) temporary
    (B) profitable
    (C) difficult
    (D) illegal

5. _____

When businesses hire an accounting firm to *audit* their financial records, they hope the accountants will not find big mistakes.

6. (A) examine and verify the accounts of a business
    (B) listen carefully to the complaints of employees
    (C) copy and store the records of a business
    (D) conceal from competitors

6. _____

After some banks began charging interest rates of 20 percent and more, the legislature considered several laws to prevent such *usury*.

7. (A) excessive rates of interest
    (B) illegal business practices
    (C) generosity
    (D) confusion

7. _____

To get her new business started, Mavina Gates borrowed money from the bank, putting up her house as *collateral*.

8. (A) proof of success
    (B) a major source of customers for a business
    (C) a temporary turnover of property
    (D) property pledged as security for the repayment of a loan

8. _____

Before Lee applied for a mortgage, he used his inheritance from Aunt Molly to *liquidate* his college loans so that he would have a clean financial slate.

9. (A) combine into a more fluid state
    (B) refinance
    (C) pay off
    (D) get rid of by force or violence

9. _____

When Senator Dobbs announced that he would not run for a third term, he reminded his listeners that the *pecuniary* rewards of public service are few and that he had children to send to college.

10. (A) personal
     (B) financial
     (C) intangible
     (D) usable

10. _____

Applying Meaning

Read each sentence or short passage below. Write "correct" on the answer line if the vocabulary word has been used correctly. Write "incorrect" on the answer line if the vocabulary word has been used incorrectly.

1. Although you had to give the landlord a month's rent for security, at least it *accrued* interest while you lived in the apartment.

2. Henry Bell knew something was wrong at the factory when he heard the garbled *audit* on his answering machine.

3. Before you decide to invest in a company, you must decide if you like the location and design of its *capital*.

4. By limiting the number of cattle offered to the meat packing companies, the *cartel* of ranchers hoped to be able to raise the prices they charged.

5. My brother-in-law asked me to put up my land in Maine as *collateral* for a loan so he could finish school.

6. The actress said that she was going to sue the sleazy newspaper that *indemnified* her reputation by printing bogus pictures of her.

7. In order to *liquidate* the deceased man's debts, his survivors auctioned his estate.

8. John told me that he passed up the Raymond account. He said it might have been *lucrative*, but the Raymond people were just too hard to work with.

9. I like all of the candidate's ideas on foreign affairs. However, I think his *pecuniary* policies would destroy this country's economy.

10. After years of *usury*, the car was rusted and badly in need of repair.

1. _____

2. _____

3. _____

4. _____

5. _____

6. _____

7. _____

8. _____

9. _____

10. _____

For each word used incorrectly, write a sentence using the word properly.

_____

_____

_____

_____

_____

_____

Our Living Language

pecuniary

In many early societies, one's wealth was measured by the number of cattle the person owned. This was especially true in times and places where there was no standard currency. The Latin word for cattle was *pecus,* and it naturally became associated with wealth and money. It eventually entered the English language as *pecuniary,* meaning "having to do with money."

Cooperative Learning: Money is a word that inspires numerous slang expressions such as "bread" and "dough." Work with a partner to list as many slang expressions as you can think of for money and wealth.

The Roots -ben- *and* -mal-

Name _____

In Latin the word for good or well is *bene*. We often find it at the beginning of English words like *benefit* or similar words with "good" as part of their meaning. The Latin word *malus*, on the other hand, means "bad." It, too, is found at the beginning of many English words like *malcontent*, words with "bad" as part of their meaning. The vocabulary words in this lesson all have one of these "good" or "bad" roots.

Root	Meaning	English Word
-ben- -bene-	good, well	benign benefactor
-mal-	bad	malignant

Unlocking Meaning

Write the vocabulary word that fits each clue below. Then say the word and write a short definition. Compare your definition and pronunciation with those given on the flash card.

1. This noun came into English through the French word *malade,* meaning "sick" or "in a bad condition."

   _____

   _____

   _____

2. This verb is derived from the Middle English word *malignen,* which meant "to attack." The modern word is more narrow, with its "slanderous" connotation.

   _____

   _____

   _____

3. In this adjective, you can see the Latin word *velle,* meaning "to wish." It now suggests doing good.

   _____

   _____

   _____

Words

benediction

benefactor

benevolent

benign

malady

malaise

malevolence

malicious

malign

malignant

4. This adjective is a form of the answer to number 2, but it is usually used in a medical context.

_____

_____

_____

5. The literal meaning of the roots in this noun are "bad ease." You can see the French word *aise* meaning "ease" in this word.

_____

_____

_____

6. This noun might name someone who gives a big donation to a school or hospital.

_____

_____

_____

7. This word is the adjective form of *malice*. It can be used to describe gossip or someone's intentions.

_____

_____

_____

8. This noun is a combination of two Latin words. One is the Latin word *dicere,* meaning "to say." This word literally means "saying good."

_____

_____

_____

9. This word is related to *benevolent,* but the word is a noun and has a "bad" meaning.

_____

_____

_____

10. If a tumor or similar growth is not cancerous, or if a smile is pleasant and friendly, we refer to it with this "good" adjective.

_____

_____

_____

Applying Meaning

Follow the directions below to write a sentence using a vocabulary word.

1. Complete this sentence: With the help of a *benevolent* wind, the sailboat _____."

   _____

   _____

   _____

2. Describe the way grandparents might look at their grandchildren. Use a form of the word *benign*.

   _____

   _____

   _____

3. Use the word *benediction* in a sentence about a wedding or a funeral.

   _____

   _____

   _____

4. Write a sentence describing what a *benefactor* might do for the school she attended.

   _____

   _____

   _____

5. Write a sentence about how someone might feel after being alone and a long way from home for months. Use the word *malaise*.

   _____

   _____

   _____

Decide which word in parentheses best completes the sentence. Then write the sentence, adding the missing word.

6. His jealousy of his brother's success ate at Nick like a _____ tumor. (benevolent; malignant)

   _____

   _____

7. During the campaign, Anita Schneider attempted to _____ Mike Halligan's character by suggesting he cheated on his taxes. (benign; malign)

_____

_____

8. The mysterious _____ were apparently transmitted through-out the hotel through the heating system. (benedictions; maladies)

_____

_____

9. The _____ of the evil queen toward Snow White was dramatically portrayed in the film. (malady; malevolence)

_____

_____

10. The vandalism at the school was no small joke; it was a _____ attempt to destroy property. (malicious; malign)

_____

_____

	Bonus Word
●	**malaria**
	The word *malaria,* a disease carried by mosquitoes, got its name from
	an early belief about how this disease was transmitted. Initially, it was
	thought that the fever and chills associated with the illness were the
	result of breathing unwholesome air. Consequently, it was named for
	the Italian words for bad air, *mal aria.*
	Use Your Dictionary: Find additional words beginning with the *-mal-*
	or *-ben-* root. Write a sentence that demonstrates the meaning of each
	word you find.

Name _____

How well do you remember the words you studied in Lessons 13 through 15? Take the following test covering the words from the last three lessons.

Part 1 Choose the Correct Meaning

Each question below includes a word in capital letters, followed by four words or phrases. Choose the word or phrase that is <u>closest</u> in meaning to the word in capital letters. Write the letter for your answer on the line provided.

Sample

| **S.** FINISH | (A) enjoy | (B) complete | **S.** _____**B**_____ |
| | (C) destroy | (D) send | |

| **1.** ABRIDGE | (A) restrict | (B) prolong | **1.** _____ |
| | (C) join | (D) cancel | |

| **2.** MALADY | (A) tune | (B) quiet | **2.** _____ |
| | (C) evil intent | (D) illness | |

| **3.** LUCRATIVE | (A) foolish | (B) ridiculous | **3.** _____ |
| | (C) profitable | (D) easily disposed of | |

| **4.** ACCRUE | (A) trim | (B) grow | **4.** _____ |
| | (C) accuse | (D) watch closely | |

| **5.** BENIGN | (A) kind | (B) generous | **5.** _____ |
| | (C) simple | (D) enlarged | |

| **6.** CREED | (A) belief | (B) give up | **6.** _____ |
| | (C) credit | (D) money | |

| **7.** INDEFATIGABLE | (A) undefeated | (B) tireless | **7.** _____ |
| | (C) slender | (D) cheerful | |

| **8.** BENEDICTION | (A) addiction | (B) proverb | **8.** _____ |
| | (C) blessing | (D) inheritance | |

| **9.** LIQUIDATE | (A) melt | (B) settle accounts | **9.** _____ |
| | (C) appear in court | (D) seal | |

| **10.** CHARACTER | (A) personal qualities | (B) opinion | **10.** _____ |
| | (C) type of myth | (D) facial expression | |

Go on to next page. ➤

11. MALAISE   (A) suggestion   (B) violence   11. _____

                     (C) type of food   (D) uneasiness

12. COLLATERAL   (A) throw back   (B) gigantic   12. _____

                     (C) security for a loan   (D) high rate of interest

13. MALIGNANT   (A) harmful or evil   (B) easily bent   13. _____

                     (C) believable   (D) remorseful

14. GALVANIZE   (A) harden   (B) move to action   14. _____

                     (C) decay   (D) measure

15. PECUNIARY   (A) financial   (B) small   15. _____

                     (C) place where birds are kept   (D) risky

Part 2 Matching Words and Meanings

Match the definition in Column B with the word in Column A.
Write the letter of the correct answer on the line provided.

Column A	Column B	
16. usury	a. a group that tries to control the price of a product	16. _____
17. benevolent	b. to examine and verify	17. _____
18. indemnify	c. a quality that attracts followers	18. _____
19. audit	d. excessive interest on a loan	19. _____
20. malign	e. desiring to do good	20. _____
21. charisma	f. to protect from loss or damage	21. _____
22. renown	g. to prevent from achieving a goal	22. _____
23. frustrate	h. to slander	23. _____
24. cartel	i. honor or fame	24. _____
25. benefactor	j. a person who has given money or help	25. _____

Name _____

Lightning

Spectacular, searing, explosive, and fiery are words that attempt to **depict** the image of a bolt of lightning. Even fireworks, with their color and noise, cannot **surpass** the drama of lightning in the summer sky. The cause for these mysterious **exhibitions** of light patterns has always
5   fascinated the curious who seek to explain such things.

The Earth, like an enormous battery, leaks electricity. Electrons bleed from negatively charged areas of the Earth to the **atmosphere.** In time, clouds may build up an electrical charge 100 million times more powerful than the charge contained on the Earth below. When this charge becomes
10 stronger than the insulating air, it returns to Earth in the form of lightning.

Another source of lightning is thunderheads. These clouds are filled with moisture in the form of ice crystals. As some of the ice crystals grow larger, becoming hail, they start to fall. Within the billowing thunderhead, the falling hail **collides** against rising ice crystals and strips electrons off the
15 crystals. The result is that the upper portion of the cloud becomes positively charged, while the bottom is negatively charged. This **induces** an area of positive charge on the Earth below. Eventually, it forces the electrons from the sky to the earth. In the same way that sparks travel the points of a spark plug, electrons jump the gap. The result is lightning.

20 Lightning strikes the earth as many as 100 times every second. A single bolt of lightning may develop 3,750 million kilowatts of power, but its energy lasts only a fraction of a second. Much of the **inherent** energy in a lightning bolt is lost as heat. The peak temperature in a channel (the path a bolt of lightning travels) may be as high as 55,000 degrees
25 Fahrenheit. However, it lasts for only a few millionths of a second. Even more **impressive** is the speed at which lightning bolts can travel—as fast as 100,000 miles per second.

One of the hot spots for lightning in the United States is central Florida. Why is lightning so **prevalent** in this area? Central Florida has two of the
30 main **ingredients** for electrical storms—moist air and heat. By contrast, the state of Washington, which also has plenty of moisture, has almost no lightning storms. The reason is simply that temperatures are much lower than the tropical heat of the Sunshine State.

As fascinating as such storms are to watch, one should always seek shel-
35 ter in an electrical storm. Standing out in the open or under a tree can be very dangerous. Lightning is attracted to both tall trees and open areas. Golf courses, parks, and beaches are excellent targets for bolts from the blue. As many as one hundred Americans are killed by lightning every year. So, no matter how much one enjoys watching nature's
40 fireworks, electrical storms should always be treated with respect.

Words

atmosphere

collide

depict

exhibition

impressive

induce

ingredient

inherent

prevalent

surpass

Unlocking Meaning

Each word in this lesson's word list appears in dark type in the selection you just read. Think about how the vocabulary word is used in the selection, then write the letter for the best answer to each question.

1. Which word could best replace *depict* in line 2?
   (A) portray   (B) distort
   (C) deceive   (D) deny

     1. _____

2. Which word could best replace *surpass* in line 3?
   (A) surprise   (B) lack
   (C) limit   (D) exceed

     2. _____

3. In line 4, *exhibitions* means _____.
   (A) arrangements   (B) displays
   (C) disguises   (D) jumbles

     3. _____

4. Which word could best replace *atmosphere* in line 7?
   (A) wind   (B) air mass
   (C) tides   (D) pressure

     4. _____

5. Which word could best replace *collides* in line 14?
   (A) brushes   (B) falls
   (C) slips   (D) bumps

     5. _____

6. In line 16, the word *induces* means _____.
   (A) causes   (B) defines
   (C) determines   (D) leads

     6. _____

7. Which word could best replace *inherent* in line 22?
   (A) inherited   (B) exact
   (C) built-in   (D) irregular

     7. _____

8. Which word could best replace *impressive* in line 26?
   (A) dramatic   (B) influential
   (C) expectant   (D) ineffective

     8. _____

9. Which word could best replace *prevalent* in line 29?
   (A) unusual   (B) mild
   (C) widespread   (D) uncommon

     9. _____

10. In line 30, the word *ingredients* means _____.
    (A) opinions   (B) arguments
    (C) elements   (D) predictions

     10. _____

Name _____

Applying Meaning

Follow the directions below to write a sentence using a vocabulary word.

1. Describe the weather in the desert. Use the word *atmosphere* in your description.

_____

_____

2. Tell about a close call on the basketball court. Use any form of the word *collide* in your answer.

_____

_____

3. Think of a painting or poster you have seen and tell about it. Use the word *depict* in your sentence.

_____

_____

4. Tell about a museum display you have seen. Use any form of the word *exhibition*.

_____

_____

5. Describe an important day in your life. Use any form of the word *impressive*.

_____

_____

6. Complete the following sentence: I was able to induce my father into . . .

_____

_____

7. Tell about someone you know who has a natural ability or talent. Use the word *inherent* in your answer.

_____

_____

8. Tell about plants or animals that are found only in certain areas of the world. Use the word *prevalent* in your answer.

_____

_____

9. Describe an athletic record that was broken. Use a form of the word *surpass*.

_____

_____

10. Describe how to prepare one of your favorite foods. Use a form of the word *ingredient*.

_____

_____

Read each sentence or short passage below. Write "correct" on the answer line if the vocabulary word has been used correctly. Write "incorrect" on the answer line if the vocabulary word has been used incorrectly.

11. It was sad to see that family *depicted* from their apartment.　　　　**11.** _____

12. The young women put on an amazing *exhibition* of tap dancing.　　　　**12.** _____

13. Billowing thunderheads extend high into the *atmosphere*.　　　　**13.** _____

14. Thick vegetation was *prevalent* in the rain forest.　　　　**14.** _____

15. Janet's blond hair was *inherent* from her mother.　　　　**15.** _____

For each word used incorrectly, write a sentence using the word properly.

_____

_____

_____

_____

_____

_____

_____

_____

Mastering Meaning

As a TV weather forecaster, you must give a brief explanation of lightning storms. Write two or three paragraphs explaining the dangers of lightning and precautions to take if you are caught in a storm. Use some of the words you have studied in this lesson.

Confusing Pairs

Name _____

Having a command of a large vocabulary allows you to make clear and exact distinctions. A large vocabulary also enables you to know the difference between words that look and sound very much alike, but have important differences in their meanings. In this lesson, you will learn five pairs of words that can be easily confused because they look and sound very much alike but have different meanings.

Unlocking Meaning

Read the sentences or short passages below. Write the letter for the correct definition of the italicized vocabulary word.

The workers made *continual* complaints to the manager about the conditions in the mill. It seemed as though there was an angry letter on his desk every other day.

  1. (A) repeated frequently
     (B) going on without interruption

The *continuous* sound of the waves lapping at the side of the boat caused everyone to feel relaxed. At night everyone went to sleep immediately.

  2. (A) repeated frequently
     (B) going on without interruption

He said he knew nothing about the disappearance of the last piece of cake, but his smile *implied* that he ate it himself.

  3. (A) to conclude or reason out from evidence
     (B) to hint or suggest without stating directly

Since she kept looking at her watch and reaching for the door latch, I was forced to *infer* that she was eager to leave.

  4. (A) to conclude or reason out from evidence
     (B) to hint or suggest without stating directly

The heavy rains will *affect* the wheat crops. We can expect the price of bread to go up in the next few months.

  5. (A) to influence or change
     (B) result

The high price of bread is just one *effect* of the flood. Insurance rates are certain to go up as well.

  6. (A) to influence or change
     (B) result

Words

affect
effect

avenge
revenge

continual
continuous

disinterested
uninterested

imply
infer

1. _____

2. _____

3. _____

4. _____

5. _____

6. _____

The Northside basketball team swore they would *avenge* their humiliating defeat at the hands of their crosstown rivals at Southside. They would meet again at the end of the season, and they planned to be ready.

7. (A) to get satisfaction for a wrong

   (B) a desire to inflict an injury in return for an insult or injury

7. _____

When the final buzzer sounded, the scoreboard showed Northside had won by 24 points. Their *revenge* was complete.

8. (A) to get satisfaction for a wrong

   (B) a desire to inflict an injury in return for an insult or injury

8. _____

For the game to be fair, we need a *disinterested* referee. I do not think Mr. Clark is a good choice. His daughter plays for one of the teams.

9. (A) without interest

   (B) free from bias; impartial

9. _____

David begged me to play golf with him this weekend, but I declined. I am simply *uninterested* in hitting a ball and then chasing after it.

10. (A) without interest

    (B) free from bias; impartial

10. _____

Applying Meaning

Decide which word in parentheses best completes the sentence. Then write the sentence, adding the missing word.

1. Seeing him drive by in that expensive car and wearing his fancy leather jacket, one might easily _____ that he had won the lottery. (imply; infer)

   _____

   _____

   _____

2. The teacher promised that the absence caused by my illness would not _____ my grade. (affect; effect)

   _____

   _____

   _____

3. Instead of going to the concert with my sister, I stayed home and watched the football game. Perhaps when I understand it better, I will enjoy classical music, but right now I am simply _____. (disinterested; uninterested)

   _____

   _____

   _____

4. When the telephone rang for the fourth time, we decided to disconnect the phone. None of us could stand these _____ interruptions during dinner. (continual; continuous)

   _____

   _____

   _____

5. The sheriff feared that the citizens of the town might seek _____, so they kept the man accused of the crime under close guard. (avenge; revenge)

   _____

   _____

   _____

Read each sentence or short passage below. Write "correct" on the answer line if the vocabulary word has been used correctly. Write "incorrect" on the answer line if the vocabulary word has been used incorrectly.

6. The baby cried *continuously* for two hours before the babysitter realized the child's shoe was tied too tightly.

6. _____

7. I tried to finish the book you gave me, but after two chapters I became completely *disinterested*.

7. _____

8. The weather is certain to *effect* attendance at the picnic. Why would anyone want to be outside in a thunderstorm?

8. _____

9. Unless we speak up in opposition to that proposal, we will be *implying* that we agree with the plan.

9. _____

10. Instead of trying to get *avenge* ourselves, it is better to let the police handle things.

10. _____

For each word used incorrectly, write a sentence using the word properly.

_____

_____

_____

_____

_____

_____

_____

_____

_____

Bonus Word

malapropism

The Rivals, an 18th-century comedy by Richard Sheridan, featured a character named Mrs. Malaprop, who confuses words with similar sounds but quite dissimilar meanings. For example, at one point she exclaims, "She's as headstrong as an allegory on the banks of the Nile." The word *malapropism* has entered the language as a common noun meaning "the comical confusion of two similar words."

Work with a Partner: Write a list of malapropisms. You might try to include in a sentence some vocabulary words you have studied, such as "I asked the band to play my favorite malady."

Name _____

The Greek word *pathos* meant suffering. The *-path-* word part has entered the English language in a variety of ways. It has been added to the ends of some words to mean a type of disorder, as in *psychopath,* meaning one who suffers from an extreme emotional or mental disorder. It can also mean a particular type of medical study, such as *pathology,* the study of the origins and causes of disease.

The Greek word *phobos* meant fear. In English the *-phobia-* word part usually adds the "fear" meaning to another word part or root, as in *hydrophobia,* hydro (water) + phobia (fear) = fear of water. Each vocabulary word in this lesson has one of these word parts.

Root	Meaning	English Word
-path-	suffer strong feelings	psychopath
-phobia-	fear	hydrophobia

Words
acrophobia
apathy
claustrophobia
empathy
hydrophobia
pathetic
pathology
pathos
psychopath
xenophobia

Unlocking Meaning

Write the vocabulary word that fits each clue below. Then say the word and write a short definition. Compare your definition and pronunciation with those given on the flash card.

1. This noun is often used to describe a quality of literature or art that evokes certain feelings. It was taken without change from a Greek word.

    _____

    _____

    _____

2. This noun combines the word part *-path-* with the Greek word *psyche* meaning "soul" or "spirit."

    _____

    _____

    _____

3. In this noun, you can see the Greek word *xenos,* meaning "foreign" or "strange."

    _____

    _____

    _____

4. This noun begins with the Greek word part *-a-* meaning "without." It is combined with the word part meaning "strong feelings."

_____

_____

_____

5. This word for a type of fear comes in part from the Latin word *claustrum* meaning "an enclosed place."

_____

_____

_____

6. This adjective is derived from *pathos* and is a synonym for "pitiful."

_____

_____

_____

7. This word combines the Greek prefix *en-*, which is sometimes spelled *em-*, and means "with" or "within," and the word part for "strong feelings."

_____

_____

_____

8. This word includes the familiar *-ology* ending found in the words for various studies such as geology and biology.

_____

_____

_____

9. In addition to meaning "an unnatural fear of water," this is another word for rabies, perhaps because one symptom of rabies is a watery mouth.

_____

_____

_____

10. This word begins with the same Greek word part as *acropolis,* meaning "the highest part of an ancient Greek city."

_____

_____

_____

Applying Meaning

Each question below contains a vocabulary word from this lesson. Answer each question "yes" or "no" in the space provided.

1. Would a coach want his team to be *apathetic* before a big game?

    1. _____

2. Would a *claustrophobic* person prefer working on a ranch over working in a coal mine?

    2. _____

3. Does a *pathologist* study ancient trails and migration patterns?

    3. _____

4. Would you expect a social worker to *empathize* with those he is trying to help?

    4. _____

5. Should a person with *hydrophobic* tendencies consider enlisting in the navy?

    5. _____

For each question you answered "no," write a sentence using the vocabulary word correctly.

_____

_____

_____

_____

_____

_____

Read each sentence or short passage below. Write "correct" on the answer line if the vocabulary word has been used correctly. Write "incorrect" on the answer line if the vocabulary word has been used incorrectly.

6. Some historians claim that opposition to immigration at the turn of the century was a *xenophobic* reaction to the cultural differences of the Europeans.

    6. _____

7. The magician demonstrated her *psychopathic* powers by reading the mind of several people in the audience.

    7. _____

8. The visitor declined the invitation to climb to the top of the Eiffel Tower, claiming he was *acrophobic.*

    8. _____

9. After waiting for several hours for the rain to stop, the umpires ran out of *pathos* and called the game off.

    9. _____

10. When the dog began to whimper *pathetically* at the door, Maxine took him for a walk.

    10. _____

For each word used incorrectly, write a sentence using the word properly.

_____

_____

_____

_____

_____

_____

Test-Taking Strategies

Tests of vocabulary sometimes ask you to choose a synonym for the word being tested. A synonym has the same or nearly the same meaning. For example, *inspect* is a synonym for *examine*. Sometimes the word being tested is given in a sentence. You are given four or five choices from which to select the correct synonym.

Sample

> **S.** We already had milk in the refrigerator, so it was *deleted* from the shopping list.
>   (A) removed   (B) missing   (C) chosen   (D) read
>
> S. _____**A**_____

When taking this type of test, you should look at each choice and eliminate any answers that are clearly wrong. Test makers may also try to confuse you by including words with sounds or spellings similar to the correct word's or by including antonyms, words with opposite meanings, among the choices.

Practice: Choose the <u>synonym</u> for the italicized word in each sentence. Write your choice on the answer line.

1. His *obnoxious* behavior in public caused him to lose most of his friends.
   (A) obscure   (B) pleasant
   (C) disagreeable   (D) ordinary

   1. _____

2. At the end of the meeting, the recorder provided a *recapitulation* of the discussion.
   (A) opinion   (B) contradiction
   (C) summary   (D) reminder

   2. _____

3. When the clock began to strike midnight, everyone knew it was time to *terminate* the discussion.
   (A) finish   (B) frighten
   (C) begin   (D) remove

   3. _____

Name _____

How well do you remember the words you studied in Lessons 16 through 18? Take the following test covering the words from the last three lessons.

Part 1 Choose the Correct Meaning

Each question below includes a word in capital letters, followed by four words or phrases. Choose the word or phrase that is <u>closest</u> in meaning to the word in capital letters. Write the letter for your answer on the line provided.

S. FINISH	(A) enjoy	(B) complete	**S.** ____**B**____
	(C) destroy	(D) send	

1. INDUCE   (A) tempt   (B) require   1. _____
                 (C) persuade   (D) enter

2. APATHY   (A) indifference   (B) fear of heights   2. _____
                 (C) pity   (D) type of medicine

3. INGREDIENT   (A) argument   (B) element   3. _____
                 (C) poison   (D) investigation

4. INHERENT   (A) natural   (B) receive through   4. _____
                                           a will
                 (C) false   (D) dangerous

5. AVENGE   (A) ambush   (B) flee   5. _____
                 (C) arrange   (D) repay

6. XENOPHOBIA   (A) fear of strangers   (B) fear of machinery   6. _____
                 (C) suffering   (D) emotional distress

7. COLLIDE   (A) put in order   (B) hit   7. _____
                 (C) collect   (D) cooperate

8. AFFECT   (A) flaw   (B) love   8. _____
                 (C) influence   (D) cleanse

9. PATHOS   (A) landscape   (B) pity   9. _____
                 (C) anger   (D) fear

10. IMPRESSIVE   (A) forceful   (B) flattened   10. _____
                 (C) producing awe   (D) simple

Go on to next page. ➤

11. PREVALENT   (A) common   (B) preventable   **11.** _____
(C) silly   (D) one who pretends

12. PATHOLOGY   (A) mental disorder   (B) logical argument   **12.** _____
(C) branch of medicine   (D) the study of migration

13. DEPICT   (A) tool for digging   (B) deposit   **13.** _____
(C) trust   (D) show

14. PATHETIC   (A) pitiful   (B) surprising   **14.** _____
(C) charitable   (D) famous

15. DISINTERESTED   (A) bored   (B) impartial   **15.** _____
(C) impoverished   (D) disorderly

Part 2 Matching Words and Meanings

Match the definition in Column B with the word in Column A.
Write the letter of the correct definition on the answer line.

Column A	**Column B**	
16. empathy	a. a person with a severe mental disorder	**16.** _____
17. claustrophobia	b. sharing another's feelings	**17.** _____
18. continuous	c. to conclude from an examination of evidence	**18.** _____
19. continual	d. fear of enclosed places	**19.** _____
20. acrophobia	e. without interruption	**20.** _____
21. surpass	f. a display	**21.** _____
22. infer	g. repeated frequently	**22.** _____
23. imply	h. fear of high places	**23.** _____
24. psychopath	i. to go beyond	**24.** _____
25. exhibition	j. to hint or suggest	**25.** _____

In Search of a Common Language

Name _____

For centuries, **legions** of clever linguists have attempted to create a world language. With this universal language, they hoped to **foster** good-will as well as serve the causes of international commerce and learning. None of these languages has been as successful as Esperanto. Although

5 people assume that it was an experiment that failed, Esperantists, esti-mated to number between eight million and sixteen million, are found throughout the world.

In 1887 Lazarus Ludwig Zamenhof published *Lingvo Internacia de la Doktoro Esperanto (International Language by Doctor Hopeful)*. Bialystok, Rus-

10 sia (now part of Poland), where Zamenhof grew up, was a place where numerous languages were spoken. As a result, Russians, Poles, Germans, Estonians, and Latvians **profoundly** mistrusted and misunderstood each other. Zamenhof's dream was to fashion a new language through which his neighbors could learn to coexist. His initial goals for the **nascent** lan-

15 guage were for it to be so simple and logical that anyone could learn it, and to be so neutral in political and cultural connotations that it could become everyone's second language.

Zamenhof succeeded in at least one way. The central **tenets** of Esperanto are its elegant simplicity and its **relentless** logic. In contrast to English,

20 with its sometimes bewildering spelling and pronunciation, Esperanto is strictly phonetic. Every word is pronounced exactly as it is spelled. Fur-thermore, grammar and **syntax** have been reduced to sixteen rules that have no exceptions. For example, every noun ends in *-o*, every adjective in *-a*, and every adverb in *-e*. Experts claim that even a **novice** can learn

25 the language in one hundred hours or less.

Furthermore, in keeping with his **prosaic** approach to language, Zamen-hof searched dictionaries of the Western world, choosing from each the most common roots on which to graft his new language. From only 2,000 roots, plus a variety of prefixes and suffixes, Esperantists have

30 access to a 10,000-word vocabulary.

Zamenhof's dream of establishing Esperanto as a universal second lan-guage never completely caught on. By the end of World War II, English had become the language of business, diplomacy, and science. On a smaller scale, however, Esperanto is doing the work its creator intended.

35 Countries like Japan and China use it to **facilitate** discussions between speakers of different dialects. In this way, Esperanto helps to expand communication among people who might otherwise never communi-cate at all.

Words
facilitate
foster
legion
nascent
novice
profound
prosaic
relentless
syntax
tenet

Unlocking Meaning

Each word in this lesson's word list appears in dark type in the selection you just read. Think about how the vocabulary word is used in the selection, then write the letter for the best answer to each question.

1. Which words could best replace *legions* in line 1?
   (A) reduced quantities   (B) secret organizations
   (C) limited groups   (D) large numbers

   1. _____

2. Which word could best replace *foster* in line 2?
   (A) promote   (B) conquer
   (C) transfer   (D) communicate

   2. _____

3. Which word could best replace *profoundly* in line 12?
   (A) remarkably   (B) deeply
   (C) rarely   (D) selectively

   3. _____

4. A *nascent* language (line 14) can best be described as one that is _____.
   (A) expressive   (B) coming into being
   (C) rejected as too difficult   (D) imposed on speakers

   4. _____

5. The word *tenets* (line 18) can best be explained as _____.
   (A) speculations   (B) followers
   (C) strange twists   (D) principles

   5. _____

6. Which word could best replace *relentless* in line 19?
   (A) inadequate   (B) amusing
   (C) steady   (D) mandatory

   6. _____

7. *Syntax* (line 22) can best be explained as a _____.
   (A) way words are put together to form sentences   (B) complicated theory
   (C) system for translating foreign languages   (D) demonstration of how something works

   7. _____

8. Which word or words could best replace *novice* in line 24?
   (A) expert   (B) participant
   (C) teacher   (D) beginner

   8. _____

9. Which word could best replace *prosaic* in line 26?
   (A) fictional   (B) straightforward
   (C) obscure   (D) gentle

   9. _____

10. Which word or words could best replace *facilitate* in line 35?
    (A) complicate   (B) record
    (C) make easier   (D) confuse

    10. _____

Applying Meaning

Follow the directions below to write a sentence using a vocabulary word.

1. Describe how a visitor to Washington, D.C., might react to seeing a historical monument for the first time. Use any form of the word *profound*.

   _____

   _____

   _____

2. Describe the weather on a typically bleak November day. Use any form of the word *relentless*.

   _____

   _____

   _____

3. Describe a crowd of people at a sporting event or concert. Use any form of the word *legion*.

   _____

   _____

   _____

4. Explain how you learned a new task or pursued a new interest. Use any form of the word *novice*.

   _____

   _____

   _____

5. Write a sentence describing how a gardener might help his plants grow. Use any form of the word *foster*.

   _____

   _____

   _____

Each question below contains a vocabulary word from this lesson. Answer each question "yes" or "no" in the space provided.

6. Would a professional writer be familiar with grammar and *syntax*?

   6. _____

7. Is television regarded as *nascent* technology?

   7. _____

8. Would a *prosaic* speech move its audience to take action because of its imaginative and persuasive power?

8. _____

9. Do mnemonic devices *facilitate* memorization of difficult material?

9. _____

10. Are *tenets* something that you can acquire at a store or through catalogue shopping?

10. _____

For each question you answered "no," write a sentence using the vocabulary word correctly.

_____

_____

_____

_____

_____

_____

_____

_____

_____

_____

_____

_____

_____

_____

_____

_____

Mastering Meaning

Suppose a proposal has been made to add Esperanto to the school curriculum. Write a persuasive letter to your school board, urging the members to support your stand on the proposal. Use some of the words you studied in this lesson.

Name _____

Language is made up of words, and literature is written by people who are interested in the way words work. It is not surprising, then, that we have many special words associated with language and literature. This lesson presents ten of them.

Unlocking Meaning

Read the sentences or short passages below. Write the letter for the correct definition of the italicized vocabulary word.

Jay put on a blond wig and bright red lipstick and walked around the room with a smug look on his face. His *parody* of the movie star brought roars of laughter from the audience.

   1. (A) love
       (B) exaggerated imitation
       (C) detailed description
       (D) theft of another person's ideas

Real estate salespeople hardly ever try to sell you a "house." They always use the word "home" because that word has *connotations* of warmth, coziness, and family.

   2. (A) all the meanings of a word
       (B) misleading meanings
       (C) ideas and emotions associated with a word
       (D) unusual or seldom-used meanings

Some crafty politicians purposely use slang or poor grammar in their speeches. They think such *solecisms* make them appear more "folksy."

   3. (A) unusual behavior
       (B) humorous speech
       (C) political slogans
       (D) errors in grammar or usage

Playwrights today rarely include *soliloquies* for their characters, perhaps because in real life people do not talk to themselves very much.

   4. (A) long, boring speeches
       (B) moments of decision for the main characters in a play
       (C) talking to oneself as if thinking aloud
       (D) lines spoken directly to the audience

Words
allegory
allusion
connotation
idiom
jargon
metaphor
parody
patois
solecism
soliloquy

1. _____

2. _____

3. _____

4. _____

Although she spoke excellent French, Henriette was not comfortable with the *patois* of Quebec. It was not the same as the French she had studied.

5. (A) dialect other than the standard or literary dialect
   (B) slang
   (C) rapid and mechanical style of speech
   (D) place names and landmarks of a locality

5. _____

On the surface John Bunyan's *allegory* titled *Pilgrim's Progress* is about a pilgrim's journey to a place called the Celestial City. In reality, however, the book is about a soul's journey to heaven.

6. (A) story in which animals act like humans
   (B) story in which characters stand for abstract ideas
   (C) any story about pilgrims
   (D) long narrative about a hero

6. _____

William Shakespeare is famous for his *metaphors*. Perhaps his most famous one is "All the world's a stage, and all the men and women merely players."

7. (A) figures of speech
   (B) songs
   (C) words having more than one meaning
   (D) long speeches

7. _____

Most people trying to learn English have difficulty understanding *idioms* such as "put up with" and "giving way."

8. (A) expressions in which words have different or unusual meanings
   (B) foolish remarks
   (C) thoughtless comments
   (D) types of speech used by uneducated people

8. _____

When the speaker called the candidate a modern-day Benedict Arnold, he was making an *allusion* to the infamous Revolutionary War traitor.

9. (A) vague term
   (B) accusation or threat
   (C) word that has recently entered the language
   (D) indirect reference or suggestion

9. _____

One of the hardest things about learning computers is getting familiar with the *jargon*. Words like "byte," "download," and "mouse" come up all the time.

10. _____

10. (A) titles and duties of certain people.
    (B) specialized vocabulary
    (C) code or system for communicating
    (D) humor unique to a particular group

Name _____

Applying Meaning

Decide which word in parentheses best completes the sentence. Then write
the sentence, adding the missing word.

1. The _____ of our guests from Brooklyn made it difficult to
carry on a conversation. (patois; soliloquy)

_____

_____

_____

2. When the minister began his remarks with the overused _____
"Life is a journey," I knew we were in for a long, boring talk.
(idiom; metaphor)

_____

_____

_____

3. Because our foreign visitors did not understand the _____,
when I asked them to carry out my orders they picked up the papers
and went outside. (idiom; parody)

_____

_____

_____

4. In Hamlet's famous "To be or not to be" _____, he thinks
aloud about committing suicide. (allegory; soliloquy)

_____

_____

_____

5. It was no accident that the candidate made numerous _____
to his military service, since his opponent had no such experience.
(allusions; connotations)

_____

_____

_____

6. When Steve rehearsed his speech before the school administrators, he
shocked them by using numerous _____. (connotations; solecisms)

_____

_____

_____

7. There is nothing as frustrating as having a doctor explain your illness using _____ you do not understand. (jargon; parodies)

_____

_____

_____

8. To many Americans, the word *politician* _____ smoke-filled rooms and shady deals. (alludes; connotes)

_____

_____

_____

9. In the medieval _____ *Everyman,* the title character must meet Death. All his friends, including Five Wits, Beauty, and Knowledge, desert him, but Good Deeds stays with him to the end. (allegory; parody)

_____

_____

_____

10. For my senior drama project, I am going to write and produce a _____ of *The Phantom of the Opera* called *The Fantom of the Auditorium.* (parody; patois)

_____

_____

_____

Bonus Word

shibboleth

According to the Bible, when the soldiers of Gilead captured an important crossing point over the Jordan River, they devised an unusual way to keep the enemy from using the crossing. Anyone seeking to cross the river was asked to say the word *shibboleth,* the Hebrew word for stream. Being unfamiliar with the *sh* sound in Hebrew, their enemies would pronounce it *sibboleth,* and thereby reveal their true identity. In English *shibboleth* now means a kind of password or way of using language that distinguishes one group or profession from another.

Write a List: Make a list of other shibboleths you recognize. Music, movies, and the computer fields are good sources.

Name _____

When medieval monks wanted to write, they retired to the scriptorium, a room set aside for writing and copying. The word *scriptorium,* like many other English words having to do with writing, comes from the Latin word *scribere* meaning "to write."

Words containing the Latin root *-tract-* come from the verb *trahere,* meaning "to draw" or "to pull." You see this word in *tractor* and *distraction.* The vocabulary words in this lesson all have one of these roots

Root	Meaning	English Word
-scrib- -script-	write	ascribe scripture
-tract-	draw, pull	extract

Unlocking Meaning

Write a vocabulary word for each of these definitions or clues. Then rewrite the definition in your own words. Use the flash card to check your answer.

1. to force or order into military service through a written notice; to draft

_____

_____

_____

2. a note or a series of notes written at the end of a letter; it has the prefix *post-,* meaning "after"

_____

_____

_____

3. not easily handled or moved; stubborn

_____

_____

_____

4. to assign or attribute to a cause

_____

_____

_____

Words

ascribe

conscript

detract

extract

intractable

nondescript

postscript

proscribe

protract

scripture

5. without distinctive qualities and therefore difficult to describe

_____

_____

_____

6. to draw or pull out; it has the *ex-* prefix, meaning "out"

_____

_____

_____

7. a sacred writing or book

_____

_____

_____

8. to draw out or lengthen in time

_____

_____

_____

9. to take away a desirable part; to lessen in value or importance

_____

_____

_____

10. to condemn or prohibit

_____

_____

_____

Applying Meaning

Write the vocabulary word that fits each clue below. Then write a sentence using any form of the vocabulary word correctly. You may want to use the information in the clue.

1. The Bible and the Koran are examples.

_____

_____

_____

2. The abbreviation for this word in a letter is P.S.

_____

_____

_____

3. Dentists do it to teeth. You might do it to the juice in an orange.

_____

_____

_____

4. This word could describe a house in a neighborhood of identical houses.

_____

_____

_____

Each question below contains a vocabulary word from this lesson. Answer each question "yes" or "no" in the space provided.

5. If a discussion of a problem becomes *protracted*, does it last longer?   5. _____

6. If you *ascribe* to a magazine, does it arrive in the mail?   6. _____

7. Is a volunteer army made up of *conscripts*?   7. _____

8. If a donkey is stubborn, might you call him *intractable*?   8. _____

9. If an activity is against the law, can you say it is a *proscribed* activity?   9. _____

10. Is *detraction* a synonym for subtraction?   10. _____

For each question you answered "no," write a sentence using the vocabulary word correctly.

_____

_____

_____

_____

_____

_____

_____

_____

_____

_____

_____

Our Living Language

Long ago only a few well-educated people could read and write. Consequently, the task of keeping public records and accounts was assigned to someone with these special skills. This person was called a scribe, from the Latin word *scribere*. This term was taken into English virtually unchanged around the 13th century. Like most workers, scribes occasionally hurried through their work and sometimes did not do a very good job. When this happened they were said to have "scribbled." Hence, a new word was born.

Check the Dictionary: Look up the following words in an unabridged dictionary. Try to find how the *-script-* or *-scrib-* root figures in their meaning.

scrip   scriptwriter   scrivener

Name _____

How well do you remember the words you studied in Lessons 19 through 21? Take the following test covering the words from the last three lessons.

Part 1 Complete the Sentence

Decide which definition best completes the sentence. Write the letter for your choice on the answer line.

1. If you tell a computer expert to explain something without using a lot of *jargon,* you want her to _____.

   (A) be brief and to the point
   (B) avoid technical or highly specialized words
   (C) use humor
   (D) tell her thoughts without interruption

   1. _____

2. A *nondescript* suit would _____.

   (A) look very much like every other suit
   (B) lend itself to a detailed description
   (C) probably be very expensive
   (D) have a special pocket for pencils and pens

   2. _____

3. A *prosaic* task would probably _____.

   (A) be lively and interesting
   (B) require great strength
   (C) take several days
   (D) be dull and practical

   3. _____

4. If a new law had a *profound* effect on crime, its impact was _____.

   (A) hardly noticeable
   (B) thorough and far-reaching
   (C) impossible to determine
   (D) unusual

   4. _____

5. An actor who recites a *soliloquy* would _____.

   (A) reveal his thoughts in a long speech
   (B) probably provoke laughter
   (C) speak to another character
   (D) make fun of someone or something

   5. _____

6. If an old manuscript is *ascribed* to Mark Twain, it _____.

   (A) was signed by Mark Twain
   (B) may have been stolen from Mark Twain
   (C) is assumed that Mark Twain wrote it
   (D) was addressed to Mark Twain

   6. _____

Go on to next page. ➤

7. A *novice* mechanic _____.

    (A) is an expert on new machinery

    (B) is an inexperienced beginner

    (C) refuses to learn new techniques

    (D) is an experienced expert

7. _____

8. When the teacher *proscribed* chewing gum in class, she _____.

    (A) allowed it

    (B) outlawed it

    (C) restricted it to certain areas

    (D) encouraged it

8. _____

9. When a speaker *alludes* to a historic event, he _____.

    (A) discredits it

    (B) describes it in detail

    (C) takes credit for it

    (D) makes an indirect reference to it

9. _____

10. Someone holding an *intractable* opinion on an issue _____.

    (A) stubbornly refuses to change

    (B) is uncertain about his or her position

    (C) tends to change his or her mind frequently

    (D) knows little about the issue

10. _____

Part 2· Matching Words and Meanings

Match the definition in Column B with the word in Column A.
Write the letter of the correct definition on the line provided.

Column A	Column B	
11. syntax	a. prolong	11. _____
12. facilitate	b. advance	12. _____
13. conscript	c. belief	13. _____
14. parody	d. way of putting words together in sentences	14. _____
15. nascent	e. written afterthought	15. _____
16. relentless	f. to force into service	16. _____
17. tenet	g. sacred writing	17. _____
18. protract	h. coming into being	18. _____
19. scripture	i. make easier	19. _____
20. connotation	j. implied comparison	20. _____
21. metaphor	k. steady	21. _____
22. extract	l. local form of a language	22. _____
23. patois	m. humorous imitation	23. _____
24. foster	n. implied meaning of a word	24. _____
25. postscript	o. take out by pulling	25. _____

Name _____

The Delany Sisters

The oldest living members of a **preeminent** African American family are also the oldest living authors in this country. Annie Elizabeth (Bessie) and Sarah (Sadie) Delany were 102 and 104 when they wrote *Having Our Say: The Delany Sisters' First Hundred Years.* The **annals** of their life together
5   comprise a best-selling book that offers remarkable insight into what it means to live for over a century.

Bessie and Sadie are the daughters of a man born into slavery and a woman of mixed racial parentage who was born free. Two of ten children, they lived on the campus of St. Augustine's School in Raleigh,
10 North Carolina, where their father was principal and the first elected African American bishop of the Episcopal Church. Coming from a large, racially mixed family, the Delany children thought little about color. So they were **confounded** by the racial prejudices they encountered as they ventured into the outside world. During the era of Jim
15 Crow, when segregation was enforced by legal **sanctions,** it was a shock to be **relegated** to the back of the trolley and to drinking fountains labeled "colored."

After graduating from St. Augustine's, Bessie and Sadie worked as teachers to earn money for college tuition. By 1916 they had moved to New
20 York, where Sadie enrolled at Pratt Institute and Bessie was accepted into Columbia University's School of Dentistry. At a time when few Americans, black or white, ever went beyond high school, Sadie transferred to Columbia and earned her bachelor's and master's degrees, and Bessie became the second black woman licensed to practice dentistry in New York City.

25 Each sister developed her own way of coping with the racism she encountered. Bessie, **feisty** and outspoken, believed in confrontation at any cost. As a female black dentist, she was on the front lines of double battles for equal rights. At first she refused to join her friends at sit-ins at the lunch counters of white restaurants in Harlem; however, after being
30 threatened by the Ku Klux Klan on Long Island, she became more **militant.** Sadie, more **serene** and easygoing than her sister, learned to navigate through the system. When a principal of a white school refused to hire her because he thought her southern accent would be damaging to the children, Sadie went to a speech coach. Eventually she became
35 the first African American in New York to teach domestic science on the high school level.

Still **hale** and fiercely independent, the Delany sisters handle their own finances, prepare their meals, and look after the home that they have always shared. They attribute their **longevity** to a routine of morning yoga,
40 a concoction of chopped garlic and cod liver oil, and a diet dominated by vegetables and boiled tap water.

Words
annals
confound
feisty
hale
longevity
militant
preeminent
relegate
sanction
serene

Each word in this lesson's word list appears in dark type in the selection you just read. Think about how the vocabulary word is used in the selection, then write the letter for the best answer to each question.

1. Which word could best replace *preeminent* in line 1?
   (A) familiar   (B) outstanding
   (C) simple   (D) exclusive

   1. _____

2. The word *annals* (line 4) could best be explained as _____.
   (A) historical accounts   (B) rumors
   (C) necessary lessons   (D) predictions

   2. _____

3. Which word could best replace *confounded* in line 13?
   (A) honored   (B) escaped
   (C) humbled   (D) confused

   3. _____

4. The word *sanctions* (line 15) could best be explained as _____.
   (A) arguments   (B) unexpected entanglements
   (C) authorizations   (D) announcements

   4. _____

5. Which word could best replace *relegated* in line 16?
   (A) assisted   (B) promoted
   (C) banished   (D) discarded

   5. _____

6. Which word could best replace *feisty* in line 26?
   (A) foolish   (B) quiet
   (C) clumsy   (D) quarrelsome

   6. _____

7. A *militant* (line 31) person could best be described as someone who _____.
   (A) fights for a cause   (B) avoids conflict
   (C) ignores tradition   (D) follows a leader

   7. _____

8. Which word could best replace *serene* in line 31?
   (A) spellbound   (B) calm
   (C) charitable   (D) opposite

   8. _____

9. Which word could best replace *hale* in line 37?
   (A) available   (B) vague
   (C) vigorous   (D) obedient

   9. _____

10. *Longevity* (line 39) could best be described as _____.
    (A) adaptability   (B) a quest for equal rights
    (C) standard behavior   (D) length of life

    10. _____

Applying Meaning

Decide which word in parentheses best completes the sentence. Then write the sentence, adding the missing word.

1. George Washington Carver was the first African American to take his place in the _____ of science because of his contributions to agriculture and the economy. (annals; sanctions)

   _____

   _____

   _____

2. As the moon rose over our lonely campsite, only the sound of crickets and the babbling of the stream broke the _____ night air. (hale; serene)

   _____

   _____

   _____

3. The more doctors learn about how the human body ages, the better health care they can provide to increase _____. (longevity; preeminence)

   _____

   _____

   _____

4. The intricate plots of some English mysteries can _____ even the most experienced and careful readers. (confound; relegate)

   _____

   _____

   _____

5. In foreign affairs, _____ are economic penalties imposed by one or more nations on another nation. (militants; sanctions)

   _____

   _____

   _____

Follow the directions below to write a sentence using a vocabulary word.

6. Describe the behavior of an animal that is difficult to train. Use any form of the word *feisty*.

   _____

   _____

   _____

7. Explain the fate of a favorite childhood possession. Use any form of the word *relegate*.

_____

_____

_____

8. Explain the circumstances that led to a protest. Use any form of the word *militant*.

_____

_____

_____

9. Describe the condition of someone who has been sick or injured. Use any form of the word *hale*.

_____

_____

_____

10. Describe a person's or a group's accomplishments or reputation. Use any form of the word *preeminent*.

_____

_____

_____

Mastering Meaning

Biographies and autobiographies are extremely popular because they provide fascinating insights into events, times, places, and people that we would otherwise not have known. Write a sketch about yourself, a person you know well, or a historical figure in which you reveal something special or curious. Use some of the words you studied in this lesson.

Name _____

Samuel Johnson wrote "Whereso'er I turn my view,/All is strange, yet nothing new." Our language supports Johnson's statement; it is full of words that refer to various degrees of strangeness. In this lesson you will learn ten words that deal with the strange and unusual.

Unlocking Meaning

Read the sentences or short passages below. Write the letter for the correct definition of the italicized vocabulary word.

Words
aberrant
anomaly
bizarre
deviate
eccentricity
errant
erratic
idiosyncratic
incongruous
outlandish

1. Beatrice is a brilliant musician, but her habits are so *erratic* that she may never have the discipline for a professional career.

   (A) strictly uniform
   (B) wrong or sinful
   (C) reliable
   (D) lacking consistency and regularity

2. That performer is known for her *outlandish* costumes and elaborate hairdos. In her last performance she wore her jacket backward.

   (A) conspicuously unconventional
   (B) plain or simple
   (C) offensive to decency and morality
   (D) from the wilderness or hinterland

3. When our family plays the game, we *deviate* from the instructions and give each player more turns than the rules state.

   (A) separate into parts, sections, groups, or branches
   (B) depart from a set course
   (C) misuse, break, or destroy
   (D) hide

4. The ugly characters, twisted scenery, and pointless actions in the *bizarre* movie haunted us for weeks.

   (A) foreign, imported
   (B) wicked, evil, sinister
   (C) odd, grotesque
   (D) painful

5. Emily Dickinson displayed a number of *eccentricities*. For years she wore only white dresses and rarely left her house.

   (A) odd or peculiar characteristics
   (B) childlike actions
   (C) lively personality traits
   (D) costumes

1. _____

2. _____

3. _____

4. _____

5. _____

6. I will keep Aunt Sophie's big, overstuffed chair even though it may look a little *incongruous* with the rest of my sleek, modern furniture.

(A) unreliable

(B) wild, out of control

(C) simple

(D) inconsistent or inappropriate

6. _____

7. Isabella Stewart Gardner liked to shock the proper society of Boston with *idiosyncratic* habits such as walking a tame leopard on a leash.

(A) illegal

(B) irritating

(C) peculiar

(D) dangerous

7. _____

8. *Aberrant* behavior is often the first noticeable symptom of a mental illness.

(A) unique

(B) differing from the normal

(C) attractive

(D) humorous or witty

8. _____

9. The veterinarian said that our cat, who has one green eye and one blue eye, is something of an *anomaly*.

(A) something different from the usual or expected

(B) eerie stranger

(C) something not acceptable

(D) ghostly shape

9. _____

10. Sir Gawain was an *errant* knight who was almost killed by the tricky Green Knight. If you look for trouble, you usually find it.

(A) invisible

(B) out of control

(C) lost

(D) wandering in search of an adventure

10. _____

Applying Meaning

Read each sentence or short passage below. Write "correct" on the answer line if the vocabulary word has been used correctly. Write "incorrect" on the answer line if the vocabulary word has been used incorrectly.

1. Members of the English upper class are known for their many *eccentrics*. They must feel their wealth entitles them to do anything.

1. _____

2. My lab results *deviated* from those of every other member of my class, so the teacher made me do the whole experiment over.

2. _____

3. When you take a standardized test you must fill in all the *incongruous* blanks on the page.

3. _____

4. It is easier to forgive the *idiosyncrasies* of a genius if he or she accomplishes things for society.

4. _____

5. The outbreaks of the disease were so *erratic,* it was easy to predict and prepare for the next outbreak.

5. _____

6. The church held a crafts *bizarre* to raise money for the trip.

6. _____

7. "My children are *anomalies,*" laughed Mrs. DiGeorgio. "They love vegetables and they don't like sweets at all."

7. _____

8. The judge decided that the child's *aberrant* behavior called for a psychiatric evaluation.

8. _____

9. The flames in the fireplace made *errant* shadows on the castle wall.

9. _____

10. Candidates for president of the United States usually do *outlandish* things to make them seem like normal citizens.

10. _____

For each word used incorrectly, write a sentence using the word properly.

_____

_____

_____

_____

_____

_____

_____

_____

_____

_____

_____

_____

_____

_____

_____

_____

_____

_____

_____

_____

_____

_____

_____

_____

_____

_____

Cultural Literacy Note

The Weird Sisters

According to Greek and Roman mythology, a person's fortunes or misfortunes were determined by the Fates—three women sometimes called the Weird Sisters, who arbitrarily wove and cut the fabric of a person's life. The Middle English *werde* meant "fate," the control of a person's life and death. The modern word *weird* retains part of the original suggestion of "strange" or "odd."

Do Some Research: Check the mythologies of various cultures, such as the Native American and Scandinavian, to see how they explained the concept of fate.

Name _____

The Latin word *jacere* means "to throw." This word survives as the *-ject-* root in numerous English words that still retain a suggestion of "throwing." For example, if you "reject" something, you are in a sense throwing it out. Another Latin word, *tangere,* means "to touch." It too survives in many English words in slightly different forms, such as *-tang-* in *tangent* and *-tact-* in *contact.*

Root	Meaning	English Word
-ject-	to throw	conjecture
-jac-		adjacent
-tang-	to touch	tangible
-tact-		tact
-tig-		contiguous
-tin-		contingent

Words

abject

adjacent

conjecture

contiguous

contingent

intact

subjective

tact

tangent

tangible

Unlocking Meaning

A vocabulary word appears in italics in each sentence or short passage below. Find the root in the vocabulary word and think about how it is used in the passage. Then write a definition for the vocabulary word. Compare your definition with the definition on the flash card.

1. We had no way of knowing for certain how the experiment would turn out. Jason's belief that the liquid would change color was only a *conjecture.*

   _____

   _____

   _____

2. The fierce tornado uprooted trees, destroyed homes, and closed down the power plant. It seemed miraculous that the school was left *intact.*

   _____

   _____

   _____

3. She thought she knew poverty in her own city. But the cardboard shacks and open sewage canals she surveyed on her mission to Bangladesh were the most *abject* forms of poverty she had ever seen.

   _____

   _____

   _____

4. In a marathon or similar contest, the winner is easy to pick; it is the person who crosses the finish line first. Deciding the winner in figure skating or diving is much more *subjective*. Judges may differ in their opinions.

_____

_____

_____

5. Because the merchandise had been damaged, Sarah could not give the customer a refund. Giving him this news would require great *tact*. He was, after all, one of the store's best customers.

_____

_____

_____

6. The picnic is planned for Saturday at Memorial Park, but everything is *contingent* on the weather. If it rains, we will reschedule the picnic for next week.

_____

_____

_____

7. The ice-skating rink will be easy to find. Everyone knows how to get to Springside School, and the skating rink is *adjacent* to the school.

_____

_____

_____

8. The principal was not satisfied by assurances that the class was doing much better work. She wanted to see some test scores or other *tangible* results.

_____

_____

_____

9. The weather report did not include the forecasts for Alaska and Hawaii. It mentioned only the *contiguous* forty-eight states.

_____

_____

_____

10. As the sun slowly dropped in the western sky, its outline momentarily was *tangent* with the horizon.

_____

_____

_____

Applying Meaning

Read each sentence or short passage below. Write "correct" on the answer line if the vocabulary word has been used correctly. Write "incorrect" on the answer line if the vocabulary word has been used incorrectly.

1. The city council *abjects* to the mayor's plan to raise taxes.

1. _____

2. Everyone seemed confident that the club could keep expenses within the budget, but the president insisted that we have a *contingency* plan in case we run out of money.

2. _____

3. It was little wonder that Ellen would not speak to him. He showed no *tact* in talking about her brother's difficulty finding a job.

3. _____

4. The police worked in close *conjecture* with the FBI to solve the kidnapping.

4. _____

5. The water dripped *contiguously* from the broken pipe and kept us awake all night.

5. _____

6. The circular driveway in front of her house was *tangent* to the street, so we were able to squeeze into traffic.

6. _____

For each word used incorrectly, write a sentence using the word properly.

_____

_____

_____

_____

_____

_____

_____

_____

Follow the directions below to write a sentence using a vocabulary word.

7. Describe the location of your school or home. Use the word *adjacent*.

_____

_____

_____

8. Tell about something you or someone you know has managed to preserve or protect from harm. Use the word *intact*.

_____

_____

_____

9. State an opinion or belief you hold or someone you know holds on an issue. Use the word *subjective*.

_____

_____

_____

10. Describe a prize or award you or someone you know received. Use the word *tangible*.

_____

_____

_____

Cultural Literacy Note

Achilles' Heel

Achilles is one of the most famous warriors in Greek mythology, but he had one weakness. When he was born, his mother dipped him into the River Styx, so that the sacred water would make him invulnerable. Unfortunately, she held him by his heel and therefore left him with one vulnerable spot. In the final year of the Trojan War, Achilles received a mortal wound in his heel.

Today if you refer to someone's Achilles' heel you are talking about his or her one weakness. Mathematics might be one student's Achilles' heel. Pitching may be a baseball team's Achilles' heel.

Write a Paragraph: In a short paragraph identify and explain someone's or something's Achilles' heel.

Name _____

How well do you remember the words you studied in Lessons 22 through 24? Take the following test covering the words from the last three lessons.

Choose the Correct Meaning

Each question below includes a word in capital letters, followed by four words or phrases. Choose the word or phrase that is <u>closest</u> in meaning to the word in capital letters. Write the letter for your answer on the line provided.

Sample

S. FINISH	(A) enjoy	(B) complete	**S.** ___**B**___
	(C) destroy	(D) send	

1. LONGEVITY   (A) lengthy illness   (B) scientific theory   **1.** _____
                 (C) long life   (D) easily stretched

2. OUTLANDISH   (A) normal   (B) foreign   **2.** _____
                 (C) silly   (D) outstanding

3. ERRANT   (A) wandering   (B) characterized by   **3.** _____
                                            many errors
                 (C) peculiar   (D) elderly

4. CONFOUND   (A) confuse   (B) mix together   **4.** _____
                 (C) discover   (D) arrange

5. INTACT   (A) careful   (B) fastened firmly   **5.** _____
                 (C) interesting   (D) undamaged

6. SUBJECTIVE   (A) main topic   (B) personal   **6.** _____
                 (C) underwater object   (D) illegal

7. ANOMALY   (A) something not   (B) related to the body   **7.** _____
                        normal
                 (C) misnamed   (D) liveliness

8. INCONGRUOUS   (A) grooved   (B) related to Congress   **8.** _____
                 (C) unsuited   (D) appropriate

9. HALE   (A) frozen rain   (B) vigorous   **9.** _____
                 (C) ill-tempered   (D) spiritual or saintly

10. SANCTION   (A) holy place   (B) to restrain   **10.** _____
                 (C) to calm or relax   (D) to authorize

11. MILITANT   (A) aggressive in   (B) member of the   **11.** _____
                        defending a cause   armed service
                 (C) very small portion   (D) one who studies
                                             military strategy

Go on to next page. ➤

12. DEVIATE   (A) to consume   (B) to devise   **12.** _____
(C) to guard against   (D) to depart from the expected

13. CONJECTURE   (A) a guess   (B) an overcrowded condition   **13.** _____
(C) rejection   (D) a combination or association

14. TACT   (A) type of fastener   (B) vulgarity   **14.** _____
(C) grace and diplomacy   (D) unharmed

15. TANGIBLE   (A) real and concrete   (B) unusual   **15.** _____
(C) vague and abstract   (D) tasty

16. ADJACENT   (A) thoroughly hopeless   (B) near   **16.** _____
(C) far removed   (D) adjustable

17. ERRATIC   (A) a wanderer   (B) predictable   **17.** _____
(C) inconsistent   (D) mistaken

18. RELEGATE   (A) a representative   (B) to banish   **18.** _____
(C) related to current interests   (D) to narrate

19. SERENE   (A) calm and peaceful   (B) shrill and piercing   **19.** _____
(C) heavenly   (D) nervous and agitated

20. CONTINGENT   (A) repeated regularly and frequently   (B) depending on certain conditions   **20.** _____
(C) side by side   (D) satisfied and content

21. PREEMINENT   (A) church official   (B) preferred   **21.** _____
(C) someone claiming knowledge of the future   (D) superior to all others

22. ABERRANT   (A) disgusting and repulsive   (B) simple   **22.** _____
(C) not normal   (D) abandoned

23. FEISTY   (A) lazy   (B) easily fooled   **23.** _____
(C) frisky and full of spirit   (D) young

24. CONTIGUOUS   (A) joined   (B) constant   **24.** _____
(C) slippery   (D) contradictory

25. ANNALS   (A) books published once a year   (B) chronological record of events   **25.** _____
(C) to cancel   (D) place to deposit items

Name _____

Typhoon!

The year was 1281. A giant naval force of 4,400 ships commanded by the Mongol emperor Kublai Khan, grandson of Genghis Khan, had quietly set sail from China and Korea. Their destination: Japan. The 4,400 commanders of these ships had no doubt about the purpose of this voyage.
5   Each had been given very **specific** orders—they were to attack and conquer Japan. Each commander had a part to play in this grand **conspiracy.** Even so, this huge gathering of military strength and careful planning was doomed, not by the Japanese, but by nature, which chose to **intervene.**

Strong winds and storms were not uncommon in these seas, especially in
10   August. But on this particular August day a storm struck with winds so **abnormally** strong that nearly all the Mongol ships were sunk, over 100,000 lives were lost, and the Japanese were saved from foreign conquerors. Such a powerful and fortunate occurrence was deemed by the Japanese to be the result of divine will. In gratitude, they named the
15   typhoon *kamikaze,* from *kami* (divine) and *kaze* (wind).

Few typhoons are considered to be fortunate events. Most cause great damage and destruction as they build in strength over the ocean before moving across land. What exactly is a typhoon? Typhoons and their **kindred** storms, called hurricanes when they occur in the Atlantic
20   Ocean, are the most powerful storms on earth. It is common for hurricanes to **sustain** winds of over 100 miles per hour for days. In 1992, Hurricane Andrew had winds that reached 200 miles per hour.

Typhoons and hurricanes are regularly **generated** at certain times of the year by the warm waters of the ocean. These storms begin when evapo-
25   rated sea water is drawn into the clouds and begins dropping as rain. Energy in the form of heat is released by this rain, which in turn provokes strong winds. The rotation of the earth causes the wind to travel in a large, circular pattern. The warm, moist air travels toward the center or eye of the storm, where the air pressure is low. Because the air is
30   warm, it rises, creating updrafts so fierce that they can tear the roof off a house, snap trees, and lift boats and automobiles. As if this were not enough, such strong storms often **spawn** tornadoes and torrential rains.

Hurricanes are classified by the Saffir-Simpson scale. On this scale a storm rated 1.0 is considered **minimal,** while a storm that is rated 5.0 could be
35   **catastrophic.** Before Hurricane Andrew, only three storms had been rated as level 5.0. On Labor Day, 1935, a hurricane hit the Florida Keys and caused great damage. Hurricane Camille, in 1969, was another level 5.0 hurricane, as was Hurricane Allen in 1980. But, in one way, Hurricane Andrew should probably be placed in a category by itself. Causing $30 billion
40   in damage, it was more destructive than the other three storms combined.

Words
abnormal
catastrophic
conspiracy
generate
intervene
kindred
minimal
spawn
specific
sustain

Unlocking Meaning

Each word in this lesson's word list appears in dark type in the selection you just read. Think about how the vocabulary word is used in the selection, then write the letter for the best answer to each question.

1. Which word could best replace *specific* in line 5?
   (A) unusual   (B) impossible
   (C) exact   (D) peculiar

   1. _____

2. The word *conspiracy* in line 6 means _____.
   (A) plot   (B) group
   (C) agreement   (D) naval campaign

   2. _____

3. Which word or words could best replace *intervene* in line 8?
   (A) stand aside   (B) appear
   (C) disappear   (D) interfere

   3. _____

4. The word *abnormally* in line 11 means _____.
   (A) commonly   (B) unusually
   (C) ridiculously   (D) typically

   4. _____

5. Which word could best replace *kindred* in line 19?
   (A) related   (B) kind
   (C) childlike   (D) identical

   5. _____

6. Which word could best replace *sustain* in line 21?
   (A) stop   (B) destroy
   (C) relieve   (D) support

   6. _____

7. The word *generated* in line 23 means _____.
   (A) overlooked   (B) produced
   (C) studied   (D) changed

   7. _____

8. Which word or words could best replace *spawn* in line 32?
   (A) spurn   (B) expand
   (C) bring forth   (D) spray

   8. _____

9. The word *minimal* in line 34 means _____.
   (A) pleasant   (B) least amount
   (C) large   (D) unimportant

   9. _____

10. Which word could best replace *catastrophic* in line 35?
    (A) beneficial   (B) adventurous
    (C) disastrous   (D) casual

    10. _____

Applying Meaning

Follow the directions below to write a sentence using a vocabulary word.

1. Describe a secret plan. Use the word *conspiracy*.

_____

_____

_____

2. Use any form of the word *abnormal* to describe the weather you had last winter.

_____

_____

_____

3. Use any form of the word *generate* to tell how you might raise money for a class project.

_____

_____

_____

4. Tell how a fight was stopped. Use any form of the word *intervene*.

_____

_____

_____

5. Use the word *kindred* in a sentence about someone you feel close to.

_____

_____

_____

6. Use any form of the word *catastrophic* to describe an event in history.

_____

_____

_____

Read each sentence below. Write "correct" on the answer line if the vocabulary word has been used correctly. Write "incorrect" on the answer line if the vocabulary word has been used incorrectly.

7. The recipe gave *specific* instructions on how to prepare the pizza crust.

7. _____

8. A new bridge is being planned to *spawn* the river at its narrowest point.

8. _____

9. Ralph tried to *sustain* his dog from attacking the letter carrier.

9. _____

10. Through most of the year, the desert regions of the Southwest get a *minimal* amount of rain.

10. _____

For each word used incorrectly, write a sentence using the word properly.

_____

_____

_____

_____

_____

_____

_____

_____

_____

_____

_____

_____

_____

Mastering Meaning

In a weather emergency, a warning and instructions for evacuating the area are usually given over a local radio station. Write a radio script warning of such a weather emergency in your town or city. Use some of the words you studied in this lesson.

Name _____

Suppose you suddenly get a chance to visit a foreign country. You leave almost immediately, and you know nothing of the language. What are the absolute basic phrases you would want to learn on the plane? "Please" and "thank you," surely. Most tourists also need to learn the phrase "How much?" The question "How much?" can be answered in many ways, as you will learn in this lesson on words that tell quantity and amount.

Unlocking Meaning

Read the sentences or short passages below. Write the letter for the correct definition of the italicized vocabulary word.

As Mr. Almirez wheeled his overflowing shopping cart to the grocery store checkout counter, he marveled at the *insatiable* appetites of his growing children.

1. (A) simple
   (B) not subject to suffering or pain
   (C) impossible to satisfy
   (D) characterized by sudden energy, impulsive

Peter hotly denied Irma's charge against him. "There's not even an *iota* of truth in what she says," he cried. "I never cheated."

2. (A) tiny amount
   (B) kind word
   (C) atom or group of atoms
   (D) refund

The Mississippi River continuously deposits sediment as it enters the Gulf of Mexico. This *accretion* of deposits causes the river to form fan-like deltas.

3. (A) acceleration
   (B) problem
   (C) provision of what is needed or desired
   (D) growth or enlargement through accumulation

A well-furnished parlor in Victorian times had a *plethora* of decorative items. Sometimes there were so many vases, pictures, pillows, doilies, scarves, and small trinkets that one could hardly see the furniture.

4. (A) matching sets
   (B) excess
   (C) shortage
   (D) deficiency

Words

accretion

appreciable

copious

fathomless

finite

insatiable

iota

paltry

pittance

plethora

1. _____

2. _____

3. _____

4. _____

Like the ocean depths, outer space holds *fathomless* mysteries.

5. (A) incapable of being measured or understood

   (B) inconsequential

   (C) easily explained

   (D) without foundation

5. _____

Even though Woodstock is only thirty or so miles from Plymouth, its higher elevation gives the village *appreciably* cooler temperatures.

6. (A) dangerously

   (B) noticeably

   (C) impossibly

   (D) immeasurably

6. _____

Michele tried to prove to her parents that her allowance is only a *pittance* compared to the amounts her classmates receive every week.

7. (A) fair amount

   (B) insult

   (C) small amount of money

   (D) foreign currency

7. _____

Joan took such *copious* notes in history class that she did not have time to review them all before the exam.

8. (A) simple

   (B) poorly organized

   (C) repetitious

   (D) abundant

8. _____

Ms. Fazon had hoped that Polk's Antique Shop would make a substantial donation to the charity auction. Instead, Polk's gave some *paltry* bits of china.

9. (A) meager; insignificant

   (B) new

   (C) excellent; outstanding

   (D) foul smelling

9. _____

There is a *finite* number of combinations to the safe. It may take thousands of attempts, but we will eventually find the numbers that work.

10. (A) unending; eternal

    (B) limited

    (C) constantly changing

    (D) incalculable; uncertain

10. _____

Name _____

Applying Meaning

Follow the directions below to write a sentence using a vocabulary word.

1. Describe a conversation in which many people give someone advice. Use the word *plethora* in your description.

_____

_____

_____

2. Describe a birthday present. Use any form of the word *paltry* in your description.

_____

_____

_____

3. Complete the sentence: Even though no one knows exactly how many, there is a *finite* number of ...

_____

_____

_____

4. Write a short weather forecast. Use the word *copious*.

_____

_____

_____

5. Write a sentence describing a person's salary. Use the word *pittance*.

_____

_____

_____

Decide which word in parentheses best completes the sentence. Then write the sentence, adding the missing word.

6. The Roman Empire grew by _____ until it controlled most of the lands around the Mediterranean Sea. (accretion; iota)

_____

_____

_____

7. I have seen no _____ difference in the skaters' performances since they began using a choreographer. (appreciable; finite)

_____

_____

_____

8. In the melodramatic story, the heroine gazed into the hero's _____ dark eyes. (copious; fathomless)

_____

_____

_____

9. My boss has a(n) _____ need to control every situation, no matter how trivial. (paltry; insatiable)

_____

_____

_____

10. There was not one _____ of fear in his voice as he calmly guided the rescuer. (iota; pittance)

_____

_____

_____

Our Living Language

humongous

The slang term *humongous,* meaning extremely large or gigantic, was probably formed by combining *huge* and *monstrous* or *tremendous.* Although *humongous* has not as yet been accepted as a standard English word, many commonly accepted words have been formed by combining two existing words.

motor + hotel = motel

breakfast + lunch = brunch

Cooperative Learning: Work with a partner to see how many words you can think of that are a blend of two other words, then check their history in an unabridged dictionary. Here are two hints.

smoke + fog =   **blot + botch =**

Name _____

A surprising variety of English words have their root in the Latin word *portare,* which means "to carry." Perhaps the variety is less surprising when you consider how many ways we use the word *carry.* Trucks carry loads, we carry ourselves in various ways, mammals carry their young before birth, words carry meaning. All the words in this lesson contain the root *-port-.*

Root	Meaning	English Word
-port-	carry	portage
	harbor	opportune

Unlocking Meaning

Write the vocabulary word that fits each clue below. Then say the word and write a short definition. Compare your definition and pronunciation with those given on the flash card.

1. This adjective could describe a small television with a handle, or a cordless telephone.

   _____

   _____

   _____

2. This word comes from the Latin word *comportare,* which combines the prefix *com-,* meaning "together," with the root *-port-.* The Latin word means "to bring together, to support." Now it refers to how individuals "carry" themselves.

   _____

   _____

   _____

3. This adjective might describe a person who enjoys soccer, rugby, swimming, or any kind of playful activity.

   _____

   _____

   _____

4. In this word you can see the word *folio,* meaning "leaves" or "pages."

   _____

   _____

   _____

Words

comport

deportment

opportune

portable

portage

portfolio

portly

purport

rapport

sportive

5. This word refers to one's behavior or how a person carries himself or herself. It has the prefix *de-* meaning "out" or "away."

_____

_____

_____

6. This word came to English through the Latin word *opportunus,* which described a wind that blew sailors toward port. Naturally, this word is used to describe something good.

_____

_____

_____

7. The spelling of this word might lead you to think it means "to carry one's age." However, it has more to do with carrying boats than with carrying years.

_____

_____

_____

8. This adjective can be used to describe a person with a stately bearing, but it more often is a reference to one's size.

_____

_____

_____

9. This word for a pleasant relationship comes to us through the French *rapporter,* which means "to bring back" or "to bring together."

_____

_____

_____

10. This word came to English through the French word *porporter,* meaning "to contain."

_____

_____

_____

Name _____

Applying Meaning

Follow the directions below to write a sentence using a vocabulary word.

1. Tell how someone should act at a funeral. Use any form of the verb *comport*.

_____

_____

_____

2. Describe the relationship between a coach and the members of a team. Use the word *rapport*.

_____

_____

_____

3. Use any form of the word *portage* in a sentence about a camping trip.

_____

_____

_____

4. Describe a telephone that does not need a cord. Use the word *portable*.

_____

_____

_____

5. Write a sentence about an artist's work. Use the word *portfolio*.

_____

_____

_____

Decide which word in parentheses best completes the sentence. Then write the sentence, adding the missing word.

6. The editor changed Manny's description of the famous opera singer from "fat" to "_____." (portly; sportive)

_____

_____

7. The new doctor on the staff _____ to have experience in five or six highly specialized fields. (comports; purports)

_____

_____

8. I am waiting for a(n) _____ moment to tell my mother about my grade on the test. (opportune; portable)

_____

_____

9. Today report cards contain comments on children's social skills. Your grandparents may have been graded on their _____ . (deportment; opportunism)

_____

_____

10. The soft drink industry often produces commercials in which _____ young people work up a thirst playing volleyball or football. (sportive, portly)

_____

_____

Test-Taking Strategies

Some college entrance examinations contain antonym questions. These questions ask you to choose the word that means the <u>opposite</u> of a word in capital letters.

Sample

| S. PUNISH: | (A) reward | (B) discipline | | | S. ____A____ |
| | (C) propel | (D) obtain | (E) compensate | |

Always read all of the choices before deciding on your answer. Think of the definition of the given word and then think of the opposite of that definition. Often tests will include a synonym as one of the answers. Do not allow this to confuse you.

Remember that words often have multiple meanings. If you do not find an opposite for the first meaning you think of, consider other meanings. Can you tell why A is the correct answer in the sample?

Practice: On the blank write the letter for the word most nearly opposite in meaning to the underlined word.

1. HALCYON: (A) foul (B) hearty (C) impoverished (D) calm (E) foolish   1. _____

2. MORTIFY: (A) embarrass (B) degrade (C) disperse (D) glorify (E) indulge   2. _____

3. INCUMBENT: (A) delegate (B) challenger (C) criminal (D) adherence (E) officer   3. _____

Name _____

How well do you remember the words you studied in Lessons 25 through 27? Take the following test covering the words from the last three lessons.

Part 1 Antonyms

Each question below includes a word in capital letters, followed by four words or phrases. Choose the word or phrase that is most nearly <u>opposite</u> in meaning to the word in capital letters. Consider all choices before deciding on your answer. Write the letter for your answer on the line provided.

Sample

S. GOOD	(A) simple	(B) bad	**S.**	**B**
	(C) able	(D) fast		

1. COPIOUS	(A) limited	(B) remarkable	**1.** _____
	(C) generous	(D) visible	
2. SUSTAIN	(A) spoil	(B) hinder	**2.** _____
	(C) clean	(D) hold dear	
3. ABNORMAL	(A) weird	(B) rowdy	**3.** _____
	(C) calm	(D) typical	
4. OPPORTUNE	(A) strange sounds	(B) unfortunate	**4.** _____
	(C) of poor quality	(D) imaginary	
5. PORTABLE	(A) imported	(B) careless	**5.** _____
	(C) immovable	(D) heavy	
6. RAPPORT	(A) quiet	(B) requirement	**6.** _____
	(C) stately manner	(D) incompatibility	
7. INTERVENE	(A) ignore	(B) entangle	**7.** _____
	(C) release	(D) interrupt	
8. GENERATE	(A) imagine	(B) arouse	**8.** _____
	(C) simplify	(D) halt	
9. INSATIABLE	(A) easily satisfied	(B) inflated	**9.** _____
	(C) greedy	(D) insane	
10. PALTRY	(A) trivial	(B) important	**10.** _____
	(C) attractive	(D) unpaved	

Go on to next page. ➤

11. SPECIFIC   (A) vague   (B) exact   11. _____
(C) special   (D) narrow

12. MINIMAL   (A) remarkable   (B) complex   12. _____
(C) maximum   (D) foreign

13. PORTLY   (A) protected   (B) exposed   13. _____
(C) hidden   (D) lean

14. PLETHORA   (A) abundance   (B) prehistoric   14. _____
(C) modern   (D) shortage

15. SPORTIVE   (A) lifeless   (B) athletic   15. _____
(C) tendency to cheat   (D) humble

Part 2 Matching Words and Meanings

Match the definition in Column B with the word in Column A.
Write the letter of the correct definition on the line provided.

Column A   **Column B**

16. finite   a. immeasurable   16 _____

17. deportment   b. carrying case   17. _____

18. conspiracy   c. noticeable   18. _____

19. kindred   d. limited   19. _____

20. spawn   e. related   20. _____

21. pittance   f. to claim   21. _____

22. fathomless   g. conduct   22. _____

23. appreciable   h. to produce   23. _____

24. portfolio   i. plot   24. _____

25. purport   j. tiny amount   25. _____

Name _____

Street Art

With the rapid spread of industry and the **ensuing** transformation of the urban landscape, city dwellers have found themselves living in increasingly bleak surroundings. Graffiti writers, in their attempts to adorn the bare walls of their environment, have become the **scourge** of politicians
5   and police. Under the **aegis** of neighborhood planning boards and even some mayors, however, what was once vandalism is now being converted into community art.

Many wall-writers, tired of **wielding** spray-paint cans and dodging police, have, on their own, branched into safer and more **remunerative** forms
10 of art. Some have redirected their efforts from buildings, bridges, and fences to tee shirts, theatrical stage sets, and compact disc covers. Others have adapted their messages to advertising, gracing the walls of commercial establishments with graffiti-style signs.

It is the **amnesty** programs for graffiti writers that have been most suc-
15 cessful at turning eyesores into art. In many large cities, former scrawlers now work to beautify the walls they once **ravaged.** Part government agency, part social service organization, and part art workshop, each group paints its town in rich **hues** while learning discipline, responsibility, and cooperation.

20 The street artists begin by obtaining the necessary permission to use unsightly fences, abandoned buildings, and blank walls as the canvases for astonishing murals. They seek ideas from local residents so that the paintings will reflect neighborhood heritage and values. Hours of effort are required to turn a vision into reality. Once the design conception is
25 **refined,** graffiti writers and neighborhood volunteers erect a scaffold, scrape and whitewash the surface, and create a grid for the sketch. Professional artists may be hired to transfer the design to the larger surface, but it is the ex–wall writers and members of the community who add the color and the detail to exotic tropical gardens, portraits of **illustrious**
30 sports stars, and memorable scenes from history.

Each of the murals is a treasured asset and a source of pride for its neighborhood. Like giant postcards or living museum walls, these murals carry a message that everyone can understand. By channeling the talents of graffiti artists into community art, color triumphs over
35 drabness in constructive self-expression.

Words

aegis

amnesty

ensue

hue

illustrious

ravage

refine

remunerative

scourge

wield

Unlocking Meaning

Each word in this lesson's word list appears in dark type in the selection you just read. Think about how the vocabulary word is used in the selection, then write the letter for the best answer to each question.

1. Which word or words could best replace *ensuing* in line 1?
   (A) resulting
   (B) spiritual
   (C) inspiring
   (D) fully disclosed

   1. _____

2. Which word or words could best replace *scourge* in line 4?
   (A) political cause
   (B) inspiration
   (C) legal setback
   (D) cause of widespread distress

   2. _____

3. *Aegis* (line 5) could best be replaced by _____.
   (A) objections
   (B) sponsorship
   (C) guarantee
   (D) proposal

   3. _____

4. Which word or words could best replace *wielding* in line 8?
   (A) handling with skill
   (B) succeeding with
   (C) admiring
   (D) dispensing illegally

   4. _____

5. *Remunerative* (line 9) forms of art could best be explained as _____.
   (A) tiresome
   (B) ridiculous
   (C) profitable
   (D) repetitive

   5. _____

6. *Amnesty* programs (line 14) could best be explained as those that _____.
   (A) look foolish
   (B) are forgetful
   (C) seem pointless
   (D) pardon offenders

   6. _____

7. Which word could best replace *ravaged* in line 16?
   (A) ignored
   (B) eliminated
   (C) ruined
   (D) discovered

   7. _____

8. *Hues* (line 18) could best be described as _____.
   (A) energy waves
   (B) shades of color
   (C) intentional errors
   (D) excuses

   8. _____

9. Which word could best replace *refined* in line 25?
   (A) polished
   (B) substituted
   (C) limited
   (D) destroyed

   9. _____

10. Which word could best replace *illustrious* in line 29?
    (A) angry
    (B) dangerous
    (C) famous
    (D) retired

    10. _____

Applying Meaning

Read each sentence below. Write "correct" on the answer line if the vocabulary word has been used correctly. Write "incorrect" on the answer line if the vocabulary word has been used incorrectly.

1. In an *amnesty* program, people with parking violations will be arrested unless they pay their fines with interest.

  1. _____

2. The music of *illustrious* composers like George Gershwin and Aaron Copland continues to have universal appeal.

  2. _____

3. Under the *aegis* of the United Nations, food and medicine were sent to the earthquake victims.

  3. _____

4. People with *refined* behavior might improve their poor manners with some simple instruction in etiquette.

  4. _____

5. Elijah was offended by several of the speaker's *remunerative* statements.

  5. _____

For each word used incorrectly, write a sentence using the word properly.

_____

_____

_____

_____

_____

_____

_____

_____

_____

_____

_____

_____

Follow the directions below to write a sentence using a vocabulary word.

6. Describe a disease that has caused serious problems for people or animals. Use any form of the word *scourge*.

_____

_____

_____

7. Describe how artists or musicians use the tools of their trade. Use any form of the word *wield*.

_____

_____

_____

8. Tell about a flood or similar natural disaster. Use any form of the word *ravage*.

_____

_____

_____

9. Describe a cause and its effect. Use any form of the word *ensue*.

_____

_____

_____

10. Describe a famous painting or a beautiful scene. Use the word *hue*.

_____

_____

_____

Mastering Meaning

Choose a social issue, such as child labor or civil rights, or the theme of an administration, such as the New Frontier of John F. Kennedy or the Great Society of Lyndon Johnson. Then write a report about the success or failure of the program. Use some of the words we studied in this lesson.

Name _____

Throughout history, civilizations have been troubled by crime and criminals. From pirates and highway robbers to carjackers and computer hackers, there have always been people who, for many reasons, defy the law. In this lesson, you will learn ten words that describe crimes and the people who commit them.

Unlocking Meaning

Read the short passages below. Write the letter for the correct definition of the italicized vocabulary word.

One of the greatest fortunes in the United States was begun by a *charlatan*. With no medical background, William Rockefeller worked as a traveling medicine man, selling fake remedies for any illness.

1. (A) spokesperson
   (B) respected scientist
   (C) politician
   (D) someone falsely claiming to be an expert

The judge showed *clemency* during sentencing. Instead of sending the defendant to jail, she imposed a fine and community service.

2. (A) mercy
   (B) hostility
   (C) uprightness
   (D) self-interest

John Brown, who sought to free the slaves by military force, was found *culpable* for the crime of treason. He and a band of his followers took over an arsenal in Harpers Ferry, Virginia.

3. (A) unprepared
   (B) at fault
   (C) searching
   (D) unqualified

The *culprit* responsible for the neighborhood graffiti was led away by the police. He was arrested as he tried to dispose of three cans of neon-colored spray paint.

4. (A) person least likely to be suspected
   (B) respectable citizen
   (C) candidate for office
   (D) person accused or found guilty of an offense

Words
charlatan
clemency
culpable
culprit
exonerate
extort
felony
incorrigible
pilfer
reprobate

1. _____

2. _____

3. _____

4. _____

Although some historians have theorized that Ethel and Julius Rosenberg were innocent victims of hysteria against Communists, the couple has never been *exonerated*. They were executed in 1953 as convicted spies for the Soviet Union.

5. (A) thrust aside

5. _____

   (B) assured of fame

   (C) proven blameless

   (D) dismissed as unworthy

One technique that the gang used to build its power was to *extort* money from shopkeepers. Even though tradespeople found it difficult to afford the weekly payments, it was cheaper to pay for protection than to risk the destruction of their stores by the gang.

6. (A) obtain something through force or threats

6. _____

   (B) encourage voluntary donation

   (C) misinterpret the need for

   (D) cleverly coax

Although its worth has never actually been determined, the *Mona Lisa* is probably the most valuable object ever stolen. It disappeared from the Louvre museum in Paris on August 21, 1911, and was recovered in Italy in 1913. Vincenzo Perruggia was convicted of the *felony*.

7. (A) amusing blunder

7. _____

   (B) source of the trouble

   (C) serious crime

   (D) minor violation

The writers Zelda and F. Scott Fitzgerald were *incorrigible* pranksters. From splashing in public fountains to turning cartwheels and somersaults down crowded city streets, there seemed to be no end to their bad habits and zany behavior.

8. (A) capable of being misinterpreted

8. _____

   (B) serious-minded

   (C) incapable of being reformed

   (D) easily reformed

It made sense to Mark that many embezzlers, who steal huge amounts of money entrusted to their care, probably started small. He imagined that they might begin by *pilfering* from their mother's purse or a sister's piggy bank.

9. (A) borrowing

9. _____

   (B) stealing small sums

   (C) acquiring in major installments

   (D) suffering a loss

The ease with which Griffin lies and cheats indicates that he is a *reprobate*. Even his own family cannot trust him to know the difference between right and wrong.

10. (A) morally unprincipled or wicked person

10. _____

   (B) one who possesses large amounts of property

   (C) person who excels at games of chance

   (D) discourteous individual

Applying Meaning

Read each sentence or short passage below. Write "correct" on the answer line if the vocabulary word has been used correctly. Write "incorrect" on the answer line if the vocabulary word has been used incorrectly.

1. Receiving a minimum sentence of ten years, the jewel thief was *exonerated* for the robbery.

   1. _____

2. Mother couldn't figure out where all the socks had gone. She was amazed to learn that the *culprit* was the family dog.

   2. _____

3. The famous doctor, praised as an important *charlatan,* received an award for her contributions to medicine.

   3. _____

4. Even though the defense attorney pleaded for *clemency* for the seventy-year-old grandmother, the judge decided to make an example of her and issued the maximum penalty.

   4. _____

5. Having devoted her entire life to helping the poor and the sick, Mother Teresa has proven herself to be a devoted *reprobate.*

   5. _____

For each word used incorrectly, write a sentence using the word properly.

_____

_____

_____

_____

_____

_____

_____

_____

_____

_____

_____

Decide which word in parentheses best completes the sentence. Then write the sentence, adding the missing word.

6. The class officers finally discovered the year-long _____ of the graduation gift fund. (extortion; pilferage)

_____

_____

_____

7. The _____ of those involved in selling secrets to the enemy is undeniable. (clemency; culpability)

_____

_____

_____

8. "Obedience school will change your pup's _____ behavior," the trainer argued persuasively. (culpable; incorrigible)

_____

_____

_____

9. By demanding part of his classmates' lunches in return for his promise not to hurt them, the bully had begun a campaign of _____. (extortion; pilferage)

_____

_____

_____

10. Although never arrested or imprisoned for their _____ activities, the gangsters were believed to be responsible for several murders. (felonious; incorrigible)

_____

_____

_____

●	**Bonus Word**
	abet
	Abet, meaning "to instigate or encourage someone to act, often wrongfully," comes from the sport of bearbaiting that was popular in fourteenth- and fifteenth-century England. In bearbaiting, a bear, starved to ensure its viciousness, was chained to a stake or placed in a pit. A pack of dogs was set loose on it in a fight usually to the death. Spectators who urged the dogs on were said to abet them, *abet* being a form of the Old French word *abeter,* meaning "to bait or to hound on."
	Cooperative Learning: Like *abet,* many other words and expressions from sports have taken on larger meanings and usage. With a group of your classmates, brainstorm a list of these terms and expressions, such as *playing hardball* (baseball) and *sidestep* (boxing).

Lesson

30

Part A

Name _____

The roots *-mit-* and *-mis-* come from the Latin word *mittere,* meaning "to send." When combined with different prefixes and suffixes, these roots give us a number of words like the ones in this lesson. Each word has something to do with sending.

Root	Meaning	English Word
-mit-	to send	emit, intermittent
-mis-		missive, premise

Unlocking Meaning

Write the vocabulary word that fits each clue below. Then say the word and write a short definition. Compare your definition and pronunciation with those given on the flash card.

1. This word is always a noun. An ambassador to another country may play this role. It begins with the prefix *e-,* meaning "out."

   _____

   _____

   _____

2. This adjective has a prefix that means "at intervals." The telephone might provide this kind of interruption to your work.

   _____

   _____

   _____

3. President Lincoln did this to slaves following the Civil War. It contains the Latin root *-manu-,* meaning "hand."

   _____

   _____

   _____

4. This noun has a prefix that means "back." If the symptoms of a disease subside, a person might be described as being in this condition.

   _____

   _____

   _____

Words

emissary

emit

intermittent

manumit

missive

omission

premise

remission

transmit

unremitting

5. It might take time to read one of these from a friend. It came into English through the Latin *missivus,* meaning "sent."

_____

_____

_____

6. This verb has a prefix that means "across." Telegraph and facsimile machines do this to messages.

_____

_____

_____

7. This noun has a prefix that means "before." If this concept is not a strong one, you may want to rethink your conclusion.

_____

_____

_____

8. Environmental clean-air laws try to prevent factories and vehicles from doing this with harmful fumes. It begins with a prefix meaning "out."

_____

_____

_____

9. This word has two prefixes; one means "not" and the other "back." The sound of crickets on a summer night could be described with this adjective.

_____

_____

_____

10. If there are too many of these, your story will not be complete. It begins with a form of the Latin prefix *ob-,* meaning "against."

_____

_____

_____

Name _____

Applying Meaning

Follow the directions below to write a sentence using a vocabulary word.

1. Describe a problem with a machine or electrical device. Use any form of the word *intermittent*.

_____

_____

_____

2. Explain how someone might convey a message without using words. Use any form of the word *transmit*.

_____

_____

_____

3. Write a sentence about nuclear energy. Use any form of the word *emit*.

_____

_____

_____

4. Write to someone who has not met your expectations in doing a job. Use any form of the word *omission*.

_____

_____

_____

5. Describe a debate on a controversial issue. Use the word *premise*.

_____

_____

_____

Each question below contains a vocabulary word from this lesson.
Answer each question "yes" or "no" in the space provided.

6. Do *unremitting* hunger and thirst continue without relief? **6.** _____

7. Can a *missive* be launched at an enemy on a battlefield? **7.** _____

8. Is *manumission* a synonym for "emancipation"? **8.** _____

9. If a mission fails and a second attempt is made, is it a *remission*?

9. _____

10. Are all emigrants foreign *emissaries*?

10. _____

For each question you answered "no," write a sentence using the vocabulary word correctly.

_____

_____

_____

_____

_____

_____

_____

_____

_____

_____

Our Living Language

Acronyms, words formed by combining the initial letters or parts of a series of words, are one way in which new words enter the language. Several well-known scientific acronyms have to do with sending out signals. *Radar* was coined from **ra**dio **d**etecting **and r**anging, *laser* comes from **l**ight **a**mplification by **s**timulated **e**mission of **r**adiation, and *quasar* was developed from **quas**i-stell**ar** objects that are powerful emitters of radio waves.

Cooperative Learning: With a partner, brainstorm a list of possible new acronyms. For example, if someone you don't like keeps smiling at you, you might tell that person to *sysel*, or **s**end **y**our **s**miles **el**sewhere. Create an acronym for several of your best ideas, and define each new word. Then present your acronyms to the class.

Name _____

How well do you remember the words you studied in Lessons 28 through 30? Take the following test covering the words from the last three lessons.

Part 1 Choose the Correct Meaning

Each question below includes a word in capital letters, followed by four words or phrases. Choose the word or phrase that is <u>closest</u> in meaning to the word in capital letters. Write the letter for your answer on the line provided.

Sample

S. FINISH	(A) enjoy	(B) complete	**S.** ____**B**____
	(C) destroy	(D) send	

1. AMNESTY	(A) accusation	(B) forgiveness	**1.** _____
	(C) decoration	(D) agreement	
2. CULPRIT	(A) fake	(B) enemy	**2.** _____
	(C) murderer	(D) lawbreaker	
3. OMISSION	(A) something left out	(B) religious trip	**3.** _____
	(C) message	(D) representative	
4. FELONY	(A) legal document	(B) serious crime	**4.** _____
	(C) argument	(D) companion	
5. CHARLATAN	(A) faker	(B) court officer	**5.** _____
	(C) healer	(D) diplomat	
6. WIELD	(A) drive	(B) join together	**6.** _____
	(C) handle	(D) destroy	
7. ILLUSTRIOUS	(A) sensible	(B) illustrated	**7.** _____
	(C) unknown	(D) famous	
8. EMIT	(A) discard	(B) give off	**8.** _____
	(C) catch	(D) explain	
9. MANUMIT	(A) legal document	(B) small crime	**9.** _____
	(C) clever trick	(D) release	
10. REFINE	(A) perfect	(B) punish	**10.** _____
	(C) ruin	(D) refer	

Go on to next page. ➤

11. REPROBATE   (A) refund   (B) threat   11. _____
                 (C) scoundrel   (D) court officer

12. AEGIS   (A) label   (B) sponsorship   12. _____
                 (C) quarrel   (D) exit

13. CULPABLE   (A) deserving blame (B) portable   13. _____
                 (C) rare   (D) unable to be
                                          reformed

14. INTERMITTENT (A) broken   (B) starting and   14. _____
                                          stopping
                 (C) seldom used   (D) secret message

15. RAVAGE   (A) uncivilized person (B) compliment   15. _____
                 (C) remarkable   (D) ruin

Part 2 Matching Words and Meanings

Match the definition in Column B with the word in Column A.
Write the letter of the correct definition on the line provided.

Column A	Column B	
16. emissary	a. steal a small amount	16. _____
17. scourge	b. shade of color	17. _____
18. hue	c. constant	18. _____
19. clemency	d. send	19. _____
20. missive	e. representative	20. _____
21. pilfer	f. take by force	21. _____
22. extort	g. cause of suffering	22. _____
23. transmit	h. declare innocent	23. _____
24. unremitting	i. letter	24. _____
25. exonerate	j. mercy	25. _____

Name _____

Jeanealogy

If you are like many people your age, the major **sartorial** decision you make each morning is which pair of jeans to wear. Well over 600 million pairs were sold in 1992 alone, making jeans the best-selling pants in the world. Denim is one of the last **legitimate** connections to our past.
5   Throughout their **hallowed** history, jeans have never gone out of style.

Blue jeans got their name long before they reached their current popularity. In the late sixteenth century, the cotton cloth used to make them was called *Genoa Fustian* after Genoa, Italy, where the material was first woven. *Genoa* was changed to *Gene* and then to *Jean* by the English, *Fustian*
10   was dropped, and the work pants made from the material were called blue jeans for their color.

The first pair of jeans were waist overalls (as opposed to bib overalls) made by Levi Strauss, a Bavarian immigrant to the United States. In 1850, Strauss went to California with bolts of brown canvas that he
15   hoped to sell as tenting to gold miners. When he realized how quickly miners' work clothes wore out, he decided to use the canvas to make **staunch** pants. After he exhausted his canvas stock, he ordered the heavy, more **versatile** fabric called *denim* from a textile company in New Hampshire.

20   Strauss's pants were enormously popular with the miners, with one exception: the pockets tore off too easily when the men filled them with lumps of ore. In 1873, he added the copper rivets that strengthen the pocket seams. Some **extrinsic** modifications followed, such as the "bird in flight" stitching on the back pockets.

25   Although we take them for granted now, jeans were not widely accepted until the late 1970s, when John Travolta wore them in *Urban Cowboy*. Designer jeans were the rage in the 1980s, when stonewashed and faded denim were introduced for those who had no time to let their jeans age gracefully. More **gratuitous** innovations were inaugurated, such as zip-
30   pers up and down the pants legs, fashionable patches in **strategic** places, and carefully designed machine rips and tears.

In spite of all the fine-tuning, basic blue jeans not only have survived, but they have triumphed. People from around the world **covet** jeans as pieces of Americana that rank with Mickey Mouse and fast food. Re-
35   cycled jeans are a hot **commodity,** often selling overseas at five times their original price. Little did Levi Strauss realize that one day his creation would clothe the world.

Words
commodity
covet
extrinsic
gratuitous
hallowed
legitimate
sartorial
staunch
strategic
versatile

Each word in this lesson's word list appears in dark type in the selection you just read. Think about how the vocabulary word is used in the selection, then write the letter for the best answer to each question.

1. Which word or words could best replace *sartorial* in line 1?   1. _____
   (A) relating to orderliness   (B) intellectual
   (C) relating to clothing   (D) quick

2. *Legitimate* (line 4) connections could best be explained as _____.   2. _____
   (A) confused   (B) genuine
   (C) current   (D) happy

3. Which word or words could best replace *hallowed* in line 5?   3. _____
   (A) highly respected   (B) perfectly conceived
   (C) suppressed   (D) remote

4. Which word or words could best replace *staunch* in line 17?   4. _____
   (A) abbreviated   (B) having delicate lines
   (C) having strong construction   (D) comfortable

5. *Versatile* (line 18) could best be explained as _____.   5. _____
   (A) conforming   (B) having distinct patterns
   (C) unusual   (D) having many uses

6. *Extrinsic* (line 23) could best be explained as _____.   6. _____
   (A) vital   (B) not essential
   (C) witty   (D) not precise

7. Which word could best replace *gratuitous* in line 29?   7. _____
   (A) unnecessary   (B) elaborate
   (C) sensitive   (D) satisfying

8. *Strategic* (line 30) could best be explained as _____.   8. _____
   (A) sensitive   (B) permissive
   (C) nearly all   (D) well-planned

9. Which word or words could best replace *covet* in line 33?   9. _____
   (A) acknowledge   (B) longingly wish for
   (C) completely refuse to   (D) tolerate
       accept

10. A *commodity* (line 35) could best be explained as _____.   10. _____
    (A) a lavish compliment   (B) an awkward situation
    (C) something bought   (D) anything seen as new
        and sold   and improved

Applying Meaning

Decide which word in parentheses best completes the sentence. Then write the sentence, adding the missing word.

1. Michael's sarcastic tone and his _____ remarks about the quality of the food would have hurt the feelings of our hostess. (gratuitous; sartorial)

   _____

   _____

   _____

2. Hattie McDaniel, the first African American to win an Academy Award for her performance in *Gone with the Wind,* was a _____ performer who could sing as well as act. (staunch; versatile)

   _____

   _____

   _____

3. Beau Brummell, known for his _____ elegance, refused to tip his hat to the ladies out of fear that he might mess up his wig. (hallowed; sartorial)

   _____

   _____

   _____

4. Although never the _____ leader of Argentina, Eva Perón had immense influence over her husband and achieved enormous popularity among her people. (extrinsic; legitimate)

   _____

   _____

   _____

5. Copies of designer merchandise, such as watches and handbags, have become important _____ to street vendors and to shoppers looking for a bargain. (commodities; strategies)

   _____

   _____

   _____

Each question below contains a vocabulary word from this lesson. Answer each question "yes" or "no" in the space provided.

6. Does a *covetous* person experience jealousy and envy?

6. _____

7. Is a *staunchly* built house apt to collapse during a storm?

7. _____

8. Are tires and seats considered to be *extrinsic* features of a car?

8. _____

9. Is devising a *strategy* one type of problem solving?

9. _____

10. Is *hallowed* ground deeply indented or full of empty spaces?

10._____

For each question you answered "no," write a sentence using the vocabulary word properly.

_____

_____

_____

_____

_____

_____

_____

_____

_____

_____

_____

_____

_____

Mastering Meaning

You have decided to enter an essay contest on the greatest invention of the twentieth century. Select an invention that is important to you, such as the personal stereo, the computer, or the zipper. Then write an essay discussing why people would find it difficult to live without this invention. Use some of the words you studied in this lesson.

Vocabulary of Discord

Name _____

Although we tend to think of discord as a situation in which hostile feelings are expressed, disagreement can often have a positive result. Differences of opinion can lead to better understanding or changed attitudes. In this lesson, you will learn ten words that deal with forms of discord and their effects.

Unlocking Meaning

Read the sentences or short passages below. Write the letter for the correct definition of the italicized vocabulary word.

The hiring of an outsider as a supervisor caused *dissension* between workers and management and interfered with productivity.

1. (A) a dramatic action or gesture
   (B) a mixture of elements
   (C) a difference of opinion
   (D) a systematic method for obtaining obedience

Two hockey players spent several crucial minutes in the penalty box as a result of their *altercation* with the referee.

2. (A) angry or heated argument
   (B) lengthy discussion
   (C) something believed or accepted as true
   (D) devastating collision

As *retribution* for offending Zeus, Sisyphus was forced to roll an enormous boulder to the top of a steep hill. Every time the boulder neared the top, it would roll back down, and Sisyphus would have to start over.

3. (A) a return to a previous state or position
   (B) a loss of freedom
   (C) the ability to remember
   (D) something demanded in payment, especially punishment

Although he never provided sufficient evidence to support the charges, Senator McCarthy managed to ruin the lives of the people he accused of being Communists. For example, many talented writers, directors, and actors found themselves *ostracized* by Hollywood and unable to find work.

4. (A) lied to and deceived
   (B) treated in a friendly manner
   (C) banished or excluded from a group
   (D) admired for patriotic actions

Words
acerbity
affront
altercation
antagonism
contentious
dissension
ostracize
pugnacious
rancor
retribution

1. _____

2. _____

3. _____

4. _____

Realizing that their *antagonism* has led to the tragic death of their children Romeo and Juliet, the Montague and Capulet families declare a tardy, sorrowful truce at the end of the play.

5. (A) regretful acknowledgment of a fault or offense
    (B) opposition or hostility
    (C) dishonest behavior
    (D) disastrous defeat

5. _____

In *Gulliver's Travels,* Jonathan Swift's *acerbity* was directed against the stupidity of people. The novel contains his bitterest denunciation of human beings.

6. (A) sharpness of mood or expression
    (B) trivial or petty thoughts
    (C) sudden, overpowering terror
    (D) powerful emotion or appetite

6. _____

Rancor was maintained by generations of Hatfields and McCoys, even though only a few members of each family could remember the original cause of the feud.

7. (A) offensive remark
    (B) bitter, long-lasting resentment
    (C) a poorly hidden feeling
    (D) something that signifies authority

7. _____

When Jack is in a *contentious* mood, he contradicts everything we say.

8. (A) free from guilt
    (B) quarrelsome
    (C) tolerant in judging others
    (D) vividly expressive

8. _____

Carmen was so defensive that she took her painting instructor's comments as an *affront* rather than as constructive criticism.

9. (A) violation of a confidence
    (B) example of an old-fashioned belief
    (C) vigorous enjoyment
    (D) intentional insult

9. _____

With his *pugnacious* temperament and his nasty attitude, Peter makes an enemy of everyone he cares about.

10. (A) independent
     (B) beyond what is normal or reasonable
     (C) ready and eager to fight
     (D) excessively dramatic

10. _____

Applying Meaning

Decide which word in parentheses best completes the sentence. Then write the sentence, adding the missing word.

1. Joseph Smith, the founder of the Mormon religion, was killed because of the _____ of a mob that wanted to see his church destroyed. (acerbity; antagonism)

   _____

   _____

   _____

2. Although she denied that she was bitter, we could hear the _____ in Denise's voice when she talked about not being invited to the banquet. (dissension; rancor)

   _____

   _____

   _____

3. The minor accident on the parkway resulted in an _____ between the two drivers, both of whom jumped out of their cars shouting and waving their fists. (affront; altercation)

   _____

   _____

   _____

4. Because he had reported the students who had vandalized the computer lab, Dwight was _____ by some of his classmates. (affronted; ostracized)

   _____

   _____

   _____

5. Many who caused _____ in the Soviet Union were sent to Siberia as their punishment. (dissension; retribution)

   _____

   _____

   _____

Write each sentence below. In the space write a form of the word in parentheses. The form of the word in parentheses may be correct.

6. Tomás de Torquemada, the first inquisitor-general of the Spanish Inquisition, was feared for the severity of his punishments as well as his _____ personality. (acerbity)

_____

_____

7. The _____ between Caligula and the Roman senators came to a head when he appointed his horse to the senate in order to humiliate them. (contentious)

_____

_____

8. Mr. Kusack sued the tabloid newspaper as _____ for the damage done to his reputation. (retribution)

_____

_____

9. The mother grizzly bear, disturbed during feeding, rose on her hind legs and roared _____. (pugnacious)

_____

_____

10. The diners _____ the waiter by leaving a tiny tip. (affront)

_____

_____

Our Living Language

The word *ostracize*, meaning "to banish or exclude from a group," comes from *ostrakon*, the Greek word for oyster shell. A vote to banish someone was a serious matter. Given that paper was scarce, the banishment ballot was written on oyster shells or pieces of tile that resembled them. It followed that the Greek word *ostrakismos* became the name of the act itself.

Write an Advice Column: Ostracism is still used today as a more subtle form of peer or social pressure. Write an advice column for teenagers in which you explain other, more effective methods for achieving unity within a group. Use some of the words you studied in this lesson.

Name _____

The roots *-pos-* and *-pon-* and the variant form *-pou-* come from the Latin word *ponere*, meaning "to put" or "to place." When combined with prefixes and suffixes, these roots give us a number of words that share a single idea. For example, both *component* and *composite* have prefixes that mean "together." Although both words share the literal idea of "putting together," they are actually very different. Whereas a *component* is a part of a whole, a *composite* is a whole made up of parts. In this lesson, you will learn ten words whose meanings have something to do with putting or placing.

Root	Meaning	English Word
-pos-	to put or place	composite
-pon-		component
-pou-		expound

Words

component

composite

disposition

exponent

expound

impostor

juxtaposition

propound

repository

supposition

Unlocking Meaning

Write the vocabulary word that fits each clue below. Then say the word and write a short definition. Compare your definition and pronunciation with those given on the flash card.

1. This word is the noun form of *dispose,* meaning "to put in order" or "to get rid of." You could think of it as putting your mood in order.

_____

_____

_____

2. It begins with the prefix *com-*, meaning "with" or "together." Its root meaning is "put together."

_____

_____

_____

3. You see the word *position* in this longer word. It is more difficult to see the Latin word *iuxta,* meaning "close by" in it.

_____

_____

_____

4. Since the verb form of this noun means "to lay oneself down," it stands to reason that this is the place where it occurs.

_____

_____

_____

5. This "phony" individual literally puts on a misleading or improper name. If you claimed to be a famous movie star, you would be one.

_____

_____

_____

6. This word came into English through the Latin *componere,* meaning "to put together." Some stereo systems are made up of these.

_____

_____

_____

7. This word begins with the prefix *ex-* meaning "out." In its literal, root sense it means someone who puts or places something out. In reality it has more to do with speaking out.

_____

_____

_____

8. It is the noun form of *suppose,* meaning "to assume to be true or accurate."

_____

_____

_____

9. This word is a synonym for *propose.* Both begin with the prefix *pro-* meaning "forward."

_____

_____

_____

10. Change the prefix to your answer to number 9 to make this word. The new prefix changes "forward" to "out" or "out of."

_____

_____

_____

Applying Meaning

Read each sentence or short passage below. Write "correct" on the answer line if the vocabulary word has been used correctly. Write "incorrect" on the answer line if the vocabulary word has been used incorrectly.

1. A collage is an artistic *composite* of materials and objects pasted over a surface.

1. _____

2. A person who *propounds* a theory dismisses it as irrelevant on the basis of its age.

2. _____

3. A bus or train station locker seems to be the favorite *repository* of shady characters intent upon stashing illegal articles.

3. _____

4. The police had to *expound* the stolen automobile until the trial could be held.

4. _____

5. As a devoted *exponent* of method acting, DeVona believes the approach to be artificial and haphazard.

5. _____

6. Buster Keaton, the slapstick comedian, was famous for his expression-less face and his gentle *disposition*.

6. _____

7. Anna Anderson, who claimed to be the youngest daughter of Czar Nicholas II of Russia, could not be entirely dismissed as an *impostor*. In 1957 a German court decided that it could neither confirm nor deny her identity.

7. _____

8. "The *juxtaposition* of the vase on top of the pedestal should allow you to fit everything into your camera frame," advised the photography instructor.

8. _____

9. According to an early *supposition*, milk in combination with any other food was considered poisonous. Obviously, this misconception was proven false long ago.

9. _____

10. Plastic, glass, and paper must be placed in separate *components* before the recycling center will accept them.

10. _____

11. Before the *disposition* of the financier's estate can take place, the will must go to a probate court to establish its validity.

11. _____

12. Alan is the company's *repository* of trademark and patent data.

12. _____

For each word used incorrectly, write a sentence using the word properly.

_____

_____

_____

_____

_____

_____

_____

_____

_____

_____

_____

_____

_____

_____

_____

_____

_____

_____

_____

_____

_____

Cultural Literacy Note

Idiomatic expressions, which are common phrases or traditional ways of saying something, rarely make sense if taken literally. For example, if you "put on the dog," you make a show of wealth or elegance. If you "put your foot in your mouth," you make an embarrassing or tactless blunder when speaking. Many of these expressions have interesting histories. For example, "putting one's best foot forward" probably originated with the ancient belief that it was unlucky to begin any journey or enterprise with the left foot. Therefore, the best foot was the right foot.

Cooperative Learning: With a partner, brainstorm a list of idiomatic expressions that begin with *put*, such as "put in a good word for someone," "put up your dukes," and "put on the spot." Write a brief explanation of the meaning for each expression. Then use an etymological dictionary of word and phrase origins to investigate the sources of the expressions.

Lessons 31-33

Name _____

How well do you remember the words you studied in Lessons 31 through 33? Take the following test covering the words from the last three lessons.

Part 1 Antonyms

Each question below includes a word in capital letters, followed by four words or phrases. Choose the word or phrase that is most nearly <u>opposite</u> in meaning to the word in capital letters. Consider all choices before deciding on your answer. Write the letter for your answer on the line provided.

Sample

S. GOOD	(A) simple	(B) bad	**S.** _____**B**_____
	(C) able	(D) fast	

1. COVET	(A) expose	(B) hide	1. _____
	(C) dislike	(D) crave	
2. DISSENSION	(A) cooperation	(B) arrangement	2. _____
	(C) declaration	(D) confrontation	
3. COMPOSITE	(A) without parts	(B) compound	3. _____
	(C) decomposed	(D) argument	
4. EXTRINSIC	(A) additional	(B) relaxed	4. _____
	(C) imported	(D) essential	
5. OSTRACIZE	(A) ignore	(B) care for	5. _____
	(C) include	(D) crush violently	
6. SUPPOSITION	(A) invitation	(B) proven fact	6. _____
	(C) interruption	(D) assumption	
7. PROPOUND	(A) withdraw	(B) release	7. _____
	(C) vigorously defend	(D) lighten	
8. VERSATILE	(A) uninformed	(B) useful	8. _____
	(C) rigid	(D) imaginary	
9. PUGNACIOUS	(A) generous	(B) smooth	9. _____
	(C) logical	(D) peaceful	
10. ANTAGONISM	(A) hostility	(B) faith	10. _____
	(C) harmony	(D) strong desire	
11. LEGITIMATE	(A) not valid	(B) despised	11. _____
	(C) theoretical	(D) ordinary	

Go on to next page. ➤

12. AFFRONT   (A) background   (B) escape   12. _____
     (C) compliment   (D) diminish

13. STAUNCH   (A) firm   (B) frail   13. _____
     (C) starched   (D) humorous

14. HALLOWED   (A) completely filled   (B) silent   14. _____
     (C) blessed   (D) condemned

15. GRATUITOUS   (A) ungrateful   (B) essential   15. _____
     (C) alarming   (D) lovable

Part 2 Matching Words and Meanings

Match the definition in Column B with the word in Column A.
Write the letter of the correct definition on the line provided.

Column A	Column B	
16. commodity	a. relating to clothes	16. _____
17. sartorial	b. something bought or sold	17. _____
18. altercation	c. mood or attitude	18. _____
19. juxtaposition	d. well-planned	19. _____
20. exponent	e. a fight	20. _____
21. component	f. explain and clarify	21. _____
22. disposition	g. side-by-side placement	22. _____
23. expound	h. one who explains and defends	23. _____
24. strategic	i. quarrelsome	24. _____
25. contentious	j. part of a larger system	25. _____

Name _____

An Early Voice for the Environment

In the 1930s, long before most people were concerned about the environment, a conservationist named Aldo Leopold sought to change America's attitude toward the natural world. From the time European settlers first set foot on the North American continent, nature had been
5   viewed as something to be tamed and used. Buffalo hides brought profit, and buffalo stood in the way of ranchers and cattle, so millions of buffalo were slaughtered. Eventually, houses were built. Land was plowed. Oil and other resources were used up. For two hundred years, decisions about the land were primarily **economic** decisions.

10 Leopold was one of the first to express **anxiety** over that kind of thinking. He knew that modern civilization had its price. Expanded highways and railroads could connect all parts of the country, but they also meant that forests had to be cut and open space destroyed. The factories and mills that provided steel and other materials for the automobile and the sky-
15 scraper also released clouds of smoke and gas and often dumped waste into rivers. Leopold was **appalled** by this devastation of the natural environment, and he worried that future generations of Americans might not have the wonder and beauty of an undisturbed land to enjoy. Once the peaceful **serenity** of open space was disturbed, he feared, it would be dif-
20 ficult if not impossible to regain.

Leopold made an important observation: As people became more and more distanced from the land, they began to lose sight of how much they depended on it. Then, he reasoned, the **converse** must also be true: If people could be brought in closer contact with the land, they would begin
25 to understand the **interdependence** between the land and its inhabitants.

Leopold was convinced that if people were brought closer with the land, they would regain an **appreciation** for the need to respect and preserve it. They could see firsthand the **myriad** interactions that exist in nature—how the quality of the soil affects the sugar maple, how the snow serves
30 to hide the meadow mouse from the birds that prey on it. In planting and harvesting a vegetable garden, they could relearn the **intricate** pattern formed by the soil-plant-animal food chain. In short, people would gain a new view of the nature around them and choose to **nurture** it rather than exploit and destroy it.

35 In his 1949 book titled *A Sand County Almanac*, Leopold recorded his experiences reclaiming a parcel of land in Sand County, Wisconsin. This book strongly influenced the nation's attitude toward the environment. While we now have many individuals and organizations concerned with the environment, this was not always the case. During his lifetime, Aldo
40 Leopold stood virtually alone in his fight to preserve nature's gifts.

Words
anxiety
appall
appreciate
converse
economic
interdependence
intricate
myriad
nurture
serenity

Unlocking Meaning

Each word in this lesson's word list appears in dark type in the selection you just read. Think about how the vocabulary word is used in the selection, then write the letter for the best answer to each question.

1. Which word or words could best replace *economic* in line 9?
   (A) educational   (B) difficult
   (C) related to money   (D) careful

   1. _____

2. Which word could best replace *anxiety* in line 10?
   (A) interest   (B) delight
   (C) joy   (D) concern

   2. _____

3. Which word could best replace *appalled* in line 16?
   (A) impressed   (B) shocked
   (C) confused   (D) amused

   3. _____

4. Which word could best replace *serenity* in line 19?
   (A) boredom   (B) calm
   (C) loneliness   (D) confusion

   4. _____

5. *Converse* in line 23 means _____.
   (A) opposite   (B) theory
   (C) logical arguments   (D) facts

   5. _____

6. Which word or words could best replace *interdependence* in line 25?
   (A) suspicion   (B) reliance on each other
   (C) independence   (D) hostility

   6. _____

7. Which word could best replace *appreciation* in line 27?
   (A) ignorance   (B) dislike
   (C) enjoyment   (D) understanding

   7. _____

8. Which word could best replace *myriad* in line 28?
   (A) rare   (B) senseless
   (C) numerous   (D) limited

   8. _____

9. Which word could best replace *intricate* in line 31?
   (A) confusing   (B) simple
   (C) orderly   (D) complex

   9. _____

10. Which word could best replace *nurture* in line 33?
    (A) support   (B) rearrange
    (C) neglect   (D) betray

    10. _____

Applying Meaning

Follow the directions below to write a sentence using a vocabulary word.

1. Tell about a time when you had to take an important test that you were not prepared to take. Use any form of the word *anxiety*.

   _____

   _____

   _____

2. Describe your reaction to a surprising event that you witnessed. Use any form of the word *appall*.

   _____

   _____

   _____

3. Describe the relationship between two countries or people. Use any form of the word *interdependence*.

   _____

   _____

   _____

4. Describe the appearance of a city or a landscape. Use the word *myriad*.

   _____

   _____

   _____

5. Describe a gardener caring for plants. Use any form of the word *nurture*.

   _____

   _____

   _____

6. Tell about a surprise party or similar event you might plan. Use any form of the word *intricate*.

   _____

   _____

   _____

Read each sentence below. Write "correct" on the answer line if the vocabulary word has been used correctly. Write "incorrect" on the answer line if the vocabulary word has been used incorrectly.

7. Where people choose to live is often a matter of *economics*.

7. _____

8. My father plans to *converse* our garage into an extra bedroom.

8. _____

9. The *serene* patient tossed and turned in her bed, called for the nurse, and finally threw a pitcher of water on the floor.

9. _____

10. After the power failure, I had a better *appreciation* of how much we depend on electricity.

10. _____

11. Teasing that huge dog the way he did showed an *appalling* lack of good sense.

11. _____

12. Hiking and fishing are good ways of getting close to *nurture*.

12. _____

For each word used incorrectly, write a sentence using the word properly.

_____

_____

_____

_____

_____

_____

_____

_____

_____

_____

_____

Mastering Meaning

Write a series of advertising slogans aimed at educating people about the need to preserve our environment. Each slogan should be no more than one sentence long. Make a poster for the one you feel is the best. Use some of the words you studied in this lesson.

Name _____

You have no doubt heard the expression "Actions speak louder than words." This lesson focuses on ten words related to strength and action. Adding these words to your vocabulary will help your words speak as loudly as your actions.

Unlocking Meaning

Read the sentences or short passages below. Write the letter for the correct definition of the italicized vocabulary word.

I have never liked high places very much. Just the thought of taking a plane trip makes my heart begin to *palpitate*.

1. (A) relax
   (B) beat rapidly
   (C) swell with pride
   (D) leap with joy

After the coach gives another rousing halftime speech, the inspired team will again *sally* onto the football field eager to take on their opponents.

2. (A) walk leisurely
   (B) ride ceremoniously
   (C) slide carelessly
   (D) rush forth

Only the most *dexterous* performer could juggle four balls while walking a tightrope.

3. (A) physically skillful
   (B) expensive
   (C) demanding
   (D) unusual

The plan to build a huge shopping center near the elementary school encountered *vehement* opposition. Parents demanded that the city council consider the danger that increased traffic would pose for their children.

4. (A) uncertain
   (B) intense and passionate
   (C) banished or excluded from a group
   (D) senseless and foolish

Words
brazen
dexterous
incursion
palpitate
redoubtable
resolute
sally
stalwart
stamina
vehement

1. _____

2. _____

3. _____

4. _____

As the election results came in, it was clear that Senator Sloan was hopelessly behind. Except for a few *stalwart* supporters, his campaign staff quickly departed.

5. (A) exhausted

   (B) uninformed

   (C) strong; loyal

   (D) weak; simple

5. _____

The Yorktown Eagles were a *redoubtable* opponent. They were taller, stronger, and more experienced. It was little wonder that they had not lost a game in three years.

6. (A) arousing fear

   (B) hated

   (C) weird

   (D) timid

6. _____

The company's threat to move its factory to another state was nothing less than a *brazen* attempt to avoid obeying environmental rules.

7. (A) clever

   (B) successful

   (C) admirable

   (D) shameless

7. _____

After three overtime periods, it was clear that the team with the most *stamina* would eventually win.

8. (A) training

   (B) endurance

   (C) loyal supporters

   (D) caution

8. _____

The mission had had numerous setbacks. Supplies had been lost or misplaced, and the workers were demoralized. Only the *resolute* courage of the leader kept hope alive.

9. (A) determined

   (B) meager

   (C) foolish

   (D) generous

9. _____

The Confederate *incursion* into the North during the Civil War was repelled at Gettysburg, Pennsylvania.

10. (A) invitation

   (B) accidental movement

   (C) retreat

   (D) invasion

10. _____

Applying Meaning

Each question below contains a vocabulary word from this lesson. Answer each question "yes" or "no" in the space provided.

1. Would someone who has a habit of making *brazen* remarks be considered polite?

1. _____

2. Is the star player on a basketball team likely to be highly *dexterous*?

2. _____

3. Does daily exercise usually increase one's *stamina*?

3. _____

4. If someone constantly changes his opinion on an issue, is he *redoubtable*?

4. _____

5. Would a *stalwart* supporter of a presidential candidate be likely to forget to vote in the election?

5. _____

6. Would bringing a loud radio into the library be considered an *incursion* by students doing their homework?

6. _____

For each question you answered "no," write a sentence using the vocabulary word correctly.

_____

_____

_____

_____

_____

_____

_____

_____

_____

_____

_____

_____

_____

_____

_____

_____

Decide which word in parentheses best completes the sentence. Then write the sentence, adding the missing word.

7. As the convicted robber was led from the courtroom, he _____ denied his guilt to the judge and jury. (dexterously; vehemently)

_____

_____

_____

8. As the forest fire came closer, you could see hundreds of prairie dogs _____ from their underground homes. (palpitate; sally)

_____

_____

_____

9. "We will put an end to government waste!" With those ____ words the senator opened the committee meeting. (dexterous; resolute)

_____

_____

_____

10. The doctor warned her that the medication might cause heart _____ . (incursions; palpitations)

_____

_____

_____

Cultural Literacy Note

Cutting the Gordian Knot

King Gordius of Phrygia is supposed to have tied a tight, complicated knot. It was predicted that whoever untied this knot would rule all of Asia. However, rather than attempt to untie it, Alexander the Great impatiently cut it with a single swing of his sword. Nowadays when we refer to "cutting the Gordian knot," we mean solving a difficult problem quickly and boldly.

Present a Report: Look through some newspapers or news magazines for an example of a proposal or decision you consider to be an attempt to "cut a Gordian knot." Report on it to the class.

Name _____

The concept of time or timing is a vital part of how we see things. The Greek word for time was *khronos.* When it began appearing in English words, the spelling was changed to -*chron*-. The word *tempus* in Latin means "time." In English it usually appears as the root -*tempor*-. Each vocabulary word in this lesson has one of these "time" roots or word parts.

Root	Meaning	English Word
-chron-	time	chronological
-tempor-		contemporary

Unlocking Meaning

A vocabulary word appears in italics in each sentence or short passage below. Find the root or word part in the vocabulary word and think about how the word is used in the passage. Then write a definition for the vocabulary word. Compare your definition with the definition on the flash card.

1. After hearing him recite his daily list of problems and criticisms, I am forced to believe Roger is just a *chronic* complainer.

   _____

   _____

   _____

2. The election could not be held for several months. In the meantime, the governor appointed Ann Kamazi to serve *pro tempore* on the commission.

   _____

   _____

   _____

3. For the rescue attempt to be a success, the helicopter and the ground crew would need to *synchronize* their efforts. If the helicopter arrived too soon, its whirling propellers would interfere with the work.

   _____

   _____

   _____

4. After photocopiers became available, carbon paper quickly became an *anachronism* in most offices.

   _____

   _____

   _____

Words

anachronism

chronic

chronicle

chronological

contemporary

extemporaneous

pro tempore

synchronize

temporal

temporize

5. The biography of Abraham Lincoln gave a *chronological* account of his life, beginning with his early years in Kentucky and ending with his assassination in Washington, D.C.

_____

_____

_____

6. Alicia was not looking forward to taking the makeup test, so she began to *temporize* with the teacher. If she could do it long enough, perhaps the final bell would ring and the test would need to be rescheduled.

_____

_____

_____

7. The church leaders urged their congregations to worry less about such *temporal* concerns as money and social status. All of these things are left behind at the end of one's life.

_____

_____

_____

8. We learned a great deal about the daily life of ordinary soldiers in the Civil War from the detailed *chronicles* many of them kept.

_____

_____

_____

9. I am not very good at making *extemporaneous* remarks. I prefer to plan my speech and answer only questions that have been submitted a day in advance.

_____

_____

_____

10. Today Van Gogh is considered one of the great postimpressionist painters. However, most of his *contemporaries* thought his art was strange and worthless.

_____

_____

_____

Applying Meaning

Rewrite each sentence or short passage below. Replace the underlined word or words with a vocabulary word or a form of a vocabulary word.

1. I was so worried about Hilary's <u>habitual</u> headaches that I advised her to see a doctor.

   _____

   _____

2. Sometimes the best picnics are the ones that are <u>unplanned</u>. Planning makes everyone expect too much.

   _____

   _____

3. The investigator asked the witness to describe the events <u>in the order in which they happened</u>.

   _____

   _____

4. The raising of the bridge was <u>coordinated</u> with the passing of the large boat.

   _____

   _____

5. The vice-chair presided <u>temporarily</u> over the discussion while the chair conferred with the senate.

   _____

   _____

Follow the directions below to write a sentence using a vocabulary word.

6. Use any form of the word *anachronism* to describe something you noticed in a picture or movie.

   _____

   _____

   _____

7. Tell how you might get out of doing an unpleasant task. Use any form of the word *temporize.*

   _____

   _____

   _____

8. Make a New Year's resolution. Use any form of the word *temporal.*

_____

_____

_____

9. Use any form of the word *chronicle* in a sentence to describe a diary.

_____

_____

_____

10. Complete the following sentence: In history class we studied the life of Thomas Jefferson and his *contemporaries,* especially . . . .

_____

_____

_____

Test-Taking Strategies

The verbal section of the PSAT and SAT tests requires you to choose a pair of words with the same relationship as another pair of words. Called analogy tests, they require you to think carefully about how two words are related and then find the word pair that <u>best</u> expresses a similar relationship.

S. FISH:WATER::	**S.** _____ **C** _____
(A) leaves:tree (B) salt:ocean	
(C) bird:air (D) earth:worm	

Remember that you are to look for the pair that is the <u>best</u> match. It may not be a perfect match. Also be careful about choices that reverse the relationship. Item D reverses the relationship you are trying to match.

Practice: Each question below consists of a related pair of words or phrases, followed by four pairs of words or phrases labeled A through D. Select the pair that best expresses the relationship in the original pair.

1. SODIUM:CHEMISTRY::   1. _____
    (A) nail:carpentry   (B) snakes:biology
    (C) textbook:history   (D) students:school

2. CRIME:RETRIBUTION::   2. _____
    (A) felony:incarceration   (B) insult:outrage
    (C) jail:misdemeanor   (D) law:jury

3. MAVERICK:INDEPENDENT::   3. _____
    (A) doctor:patient   (B) cattle:stray
    (C) incumbent:candidate   (D) vagabond:aimless

Name _____

How well do you remember the words you studied in Lessons 34 through 36? Take the following test covering the words from the last three lessons.

Part 1 Choose the Correct Meaning

Each question below includes a word in capital letters, followed by four words or phrases. Choose the word or phrase that is <u>closest</u> in meaning to the word in capital letters. Write the letter for your answer on the line provided.

Sample

S. FINISH	(A) enjoy	(B) complete	**S.** _____**B**_____
	(C) destroy	(D) send	

1. BRAZEN	(A) dull	(B) brash	**1.** _____
	(C) hardened	(D) distant	
2. ANACHRONISM	(A) type of spider	(B) Asian religion	**2.** _____
	(C) something out of its proper time	(D) inaccuracy	
3. SALLY	(A) rush forth	(B) soil	**3.** _____
	(C) delicate	(D) rearrange	
4. RESOLUTE	(A) decide	(B) determined	**4.** _____
	(C) promised	(D) arranged	
5. INTRICATE	(A) accuse	(B) simple	**5.** _____
	(C) thorough	(D) complicated	
6. PALPITATE	(A) valuable	(B) worthless	**6.** _____
	(C) flutter	(D) satisfy	
7. TEMPORAL	(A) worldly	(B) tempting	**7.** _____
	(C) ancient	(D) spiritual	
8. CHRONIC	(A) painful	(B) temporary	**8.** _____
	(C) habitual	(D) timely	
9. DEXTEROUS	(A) clumsy	(B) skillful	**9.** _____
	(C) annoying	(D) dull	
10. NURTURE	(A) nourish	(B) disregard	**10.** _____
	(C) insult	(D) starve	

Go on to next page. ➤

11. VEHEMENT   (A) evil   (B) passionate   11. _____
                               (C) poisonous   (D) slight

12. APPRECIATE   (A) answer   (B) apply   12. _____
                               (C) dislike   (D) value

13. REDOUBTABLE   (A) forgetful   (B) complete   13. _____
                               (C) reformed   (D) causing fear

14. STALWART   (A) strong   (B) clever   14. _____
                               (C) overweight   (D) weak or tame

15. TEMPORIZE   (A) tenderize   (B) evade and delay   15. _____
                               (C) reduce   (D) quicken

Part 2 Matching Words and Meanings

Match the definition in Column B with the word in Column A.
Write the letter of the correct definition on the line provided.

Column A	Column B	
16. appall	a. calm and peaceful	16. _____
17. incursion	b. invasion	17. _____
18. contemporary	c. physical strength	18. _____
19. myriad	d. shock	19. _____
20. synchronize	e. fear	20. _____
21. anxiety	f. to cause to occur at the same time	21. _____
22. extemporaneous	g. belonging to the same time period	22. _____
23. serene	h. opposite	23. _____
24. stamina	i. numerous	24. _____
25. converse	j. carried out with little preparation	25. _____

Lesson 3

fra·tri·cide (frăt′rĭ-sīd′) *n.* **1.** The act of killing one's brother or sister. **2.** A person who kills his or her brother or sister.

gen·o·cide (jĕn′ə-sīd′) *n.* The systematic killing of a national, political, racial, or cultural group.

in·ci·sive (ĭn-sī′sĭv) *adj.* Mentally sharp; cutting into; keen; penetrating. **-in·ci′sive·ly,** *adv.* **-in·ci′sive·ness,** *n.*

in·vin·ci·ble (ĭn-vĭn′sə-bəl) *adj.* Incapable of being subdued, conquered, or overcome. **-in·vin′ci·bil′i·ty,** *n.* **-in·vin′ci·bly,** *adv.*

van·quish (văng′kwĭsh, văn′-) *v.* **1.** To defeat or overcome in battle. **2.** To overcome in a contest or conflict. **3.** To gain mastery over.

Lesson 3

bel·li·cose (bĕl′ĭ-kōs′) *adj.* Inclined or eager to fight or start wars; warlike. **-bel′li·cos′i·ty** (-kŏs′ĭ-tē), *n.*

bel·lig·er·ent (bə-lĭj′ər-ənt) *adj.* Eager to fight; hostile. *-n.* A person or country that is engaged in war. **-bel·lig′er·ence,** *n.*

con·cise (kən-sīs′) *adj.* Expressing in a few words what is meant; brief and to the point; terse. **-con·cise′ly,** *adv.* **-con·cise′ness,** *n.*

e·vict (ĭ-vĭkt′) *v.* To throw out or remove (a tenant) from property by legal procedure. **-e·vic′tion,** *n.*

e·vince (ĭ-vĭns′) *v.* **e·vinced, e·vinc·ing, e·vinc·es.** To show clearly; to make evident. **-e·vinc′i·ble,** *adj.*

Lesson 2

his·tri·on·ics (hĭs′trē-ŏn′ĭks) *n.* Overly dramatic behavior or speech for effect.

la·con·ic (lə-kŏn′ĭk) *adj.* Using few words to express much; concise; terse. **-la·con′i·cal·ly,** *adv.*

po·lem·ic (pə-lĕm′ĭk) *n.* An argument or dispute often attacking a specific opinion.

trite (trīt) *adj.* **trit·er, trit·est.** Lacking freshness because of overuse; stale; hackneyed. **-trite′ness,** *n.*

ver·bos·i·ty (vər-bŏs′ĭ-tē) *adj.* The use of more words than necessary; wordiness. **-ver·bose′** , *adj.*

Lesson 2

ar·tic·u·late (är-tĭk′yə-lĭt) *adj.* Expressing oneself effectively and clearly. *-v.* (är-tĭk′yə-lāt) To state clearly and effectively. **-ar·tic′u·late·ly,** *adv.* **-ar·tic′u·la′tion,** *n.*

bra·va·do (brə-vä′dō) *n., pl.* **-dos** or **-does.** A false show of bravery.

ef·fu·sive (ĭ-fyoō′sĭv) *adj.* Showing more feeling than necessary; gushing. **-ef·fu′sive·ly,** *adv.* **-ef·fu′sive·ness,** *n.*

gar·ru·lous (găr′ə-ləs, găr′yə-) *adj.* Excessively talkative, especially about unimportant topics. **-gar′ru·lous·ly,** *adv.* **-gar′ru·lous·ness,** *n.*

glib (glĭb) *adj.* **glib·ber, glib·best.** Speaking or spoken with little thought or sincerity. **-glib′ly,** *adv.* **-glib′ness,** *n.*

Lesson 1

in·dif·fer·ence (ĭn-dĭf′ər-əns, -dĭf′rəns) *n.* **1.** Lack of interest, concern, or feeling. **2.** Lack of importance. **-in·dif′fer·ent,** *adj.*

pe·ti·tion (pə-tĭsh′ən) *v.* To ask or request formally. *-n.* A formal written request.

ruse (roōs, roōz) *n.* A trick or action intended to mislead.

suc·cinct (sək-sĭngkt′) *adj.* Concise and clearly stated. **-suc·cinct′ly,** *adv.* **-suc·cinct′ness,** *n.*

trek (trĕk) *n.* A difficult journey. *-v.* **-trekked, trek·king** To travel slowly or with difficulty.

Lesson 1

an·guish (ăng′gwĭsh) *n.* Great mental suffering or physical pain. *-v.* To suffer intense sorrow or pain.

an·ni·hi·la·tion (ə-nī′ə-lā′shən) *n.* The act or result of destroying completely. **-an·ni′hi·late,** *v.*

el·o·quent (ĕl′ə-kwənt) *adj.* **1.** Characterized by forceful and persuasive expression. **2.** Movingly expressive. **-el′o·quence,** *n.*

fe·roc·i·ty (fə-rŏs′ĭ-tē) *n.* **1.** Fierceness; extreme savagery. **2.** Extreme intensity.

ha·rangue (hə-răng′) *n.* **1.** A long, pompous speech. **2.** A tirade. *-v.* **-rangued, -rangu·ing, -rangues.** To give a harangue.

Lesson 3	Lesson 3	Lesson 2	Lesson 2	Lesson 1	Lesson 1
fratricide	bellicose	histrionics	articulate	indifference	anguish
genocide	belligerent	laconic	bravado	petition	annihilation
incisive	concise	polemic	effusive	ruse	eloquent
invincible	evict	trite	garrulous	succinct	ferocity
vanquish	evince	verbosity	glib	trek	harangue

doc·trine
(dŏk′trĭn) n. 1. A position, principle, or belief taught or held by a particular group. 2. Teachings.

in·cog·ni·to
(ĭn-kŏg-nē′tō, ĭn-kŏg′nĭ-tō′) adv. or adj. With one's identity hidden or disguised.

in·doc·tri·nate
(ĭn-dŏk′trə-nāt′) v. -nat·ed, -nat·ing, -nates. To teach a particular theory, belief, or principle. **-in·doc′tri·na′tion,** n.

or·tho·dox
(ôr′thə-dŏks′) adj. Conforming to traditional and established beliefs, attitudes, or doctrines.

par·a·dox
(păr′ə-dŏks′) n. A statement that seems to be contradictory, but may be true. **-par·a·dox′i·cal,** adj. **-par·a·dox′i·cal·ly,** adv.

ag·nos·tic
(ăg-nŏs′tĭk) n. A person who believes that the existence of God is unknown or unknowable. **-ag·nos′ti·cal·ly,** adv.

cog·no·men
(kŏg-nō′mən, kŏg′-no) n., pl. **-no·mens** or **-nom·i·na.** 1. A surname. 2. Any name, especially a nickname or epithet.

di·ag·nose
(dī′əg-nōs′, -nōz′) v. 1. to identify a disease through careful analysis. 2. To analyze the cause and nature of a problem. **-di·ag·no′sis,** n.

docile
(dŏs′əl, -īl′) adj. Easily taught, trained, or managed; submissive. **-doc′ile·ly,** adv. **-do·cil′i·ty,** n.

doc·tri·naire
(dŏk′trə-nâr′) adj. Adhering inflexibly to a practice or theory. -n. One who stubbornly adheres to a practice or theory.

men·tor
(mĕn′tôr′, -tər) n. A wise and trusted advisor or teacher.

mes·mer·ize
(mĕz′mə-rīz, mĕs′-) v. **-ized, -iz·ing, -iz·es.** 1. To hypnotize. 2. To spellbind; fascinate. **-mes′mer·i·za′tion,** n. **-mes′mer·iz′er,** n.

nem·e·sis
(nĕm′ĭ-sĭs) n., pl. **-ses** (-sēz′). 1. Something that causes one's defeat or failure. 2. One that punishes wrongdoing.

pro·crus·te·an
(prō-krŭs′tē-ən) adj. Exhibiting ruthless disregard for individual differences.

quix·ot·ic
(kwĭk-sŏt′ĭk) adj. Extravagantly chivalrous or too romantically idealistic. **-quix·ot′i·cal·ly,** adv.

bed·lam
(bĕd′ləm) n. A place or condition of uproar and confusion.

boy·cott
(boi′kŏt′) v. 1. To refuse to use, buy, or sell. -n. An organized refusal to do business with a person or group.

her·cu·le·an
(hûr′kyə-lē′ən, hûr-kyōō′lē-) adj. 1. Requiring great strength or exertion. 2. Of great strength, courage, or size.

maud·lin
(môd′lĭn) adj. Excessively or foolishly sentimental.

mav·er·ick
(măv′ər-ĭk, măv′rĭk) n. 1. An unbranded animal. 2. A person who thinks and acts independently of others in his or her group.

o·men
(ō′mən) n. A sign or happening that is supposed to foretell something good or bad.

per·ish
(pĕr′ĭsh) v. 1. To die or be destroyed, especially in a violent way. 2. To pass from existence; disappear.

shroud
(shroud) n. A cloth used to wrap a dead body for burial. -v. To hide; cover; obscure.

so·lem·ni·ty
(sə-lĕm′nĭ-tē) n. 1. Seriousness. 2. A dignified or impressive ceremony. **-so·lemn,** adj.

sub·side
(səb-sīd′) v. **-sid·ed, -sid·ing, -sides.** 1. To sink to a lower level. 2. To become quiet or less active. **-sub·si′dence,** n.

char·i·ty
(chăr′i-tē) n., pl. **-ties.** 1. The giving of help or relief to the poor. 2. Kindness or tolerance in judging others.

cher·ish
(chĕr′ĭsh) v. 1. To regard with affection; hold dear. 2. To hold in the mind; cling to.

e·merge
(ĭ-mûrj′) v. **e·merged, e·merg·ing, e·merg·es.** 1. To become visible; to come into view. 2. To rise from or as if from a fluid.

gaunt
(gônt) adj. 1. Very thin and bony; haggard. 2. Bare; grim; bleak. **-gaunt′ly,** adv. **-gaunt′ness,** n.

mal·ice
(măl′ĭs) n. The wish to harm, injure, or cause pain to another. **-ma·li′cious,** adj.

Lesson 6 doctrine	Lesson 6 agnostic	Lesson 5 mentor	Lesson 5 bedlam	Lesson 4 omen	Lesson 4 charity
Lesson 6 incognito	Lesson 6 cognomen	Lesson 5 mesmerize	Lesson 5 boycott	Lesson 4 perish	Lesson 4 cherish
Lesson 6 indoctrinate	Lesson 6 diagnose	Lesson 5 nemesis	Lesson 5 herculean	Lesson 4 shroud	Lesson 4 emerge
Lesson 6 orthodox	Lesson 6 docile	Lesson 5 procrustean	Lesson 5 maudlin	Lesson 4 solemnity	Lesson 4 gaunt
Lesson 6 paradox	Lesson 6 doctrinaire	Lesson 5 quixotic	Lesson 5 maverick	Lesson 4 subside	Lesson 4 malice

dis·cord

(dĭs′kôrd′) *n.* A lack of agreement or harmony; conflict.

---

dis·cur·sive

(dĭ-skûr′sĭv) *adj.* Wandering aimlessly from one topic to another. **-dis·cur′sive·ly,** *adv.* **-dis·cur′sive·ness,** *n.*

---

pre·cur·sor

(prĭ-kûr′sər, prē′kûr′sər) *n.* A person or thing that goes before and indicates the approach of another.

---

re·course

(rē′kôrs, -kōrs′, rĭ-kôrs′, -kōrs′) *n.* **1.** A turning to a person or thing for aid or safety. **2.** A person or thing that is turned to for aid.

---

re·cur·rent

(rĭ-kûr′ənt, -kŭr′-) *adj.* Happening or appearing again or periodically. **-re·cur′rent·ly,** *adv.*

---

ac·cord

(ə-kôrd′) *n.* An agreement; harmony. *-v.* **1.** To make agree. **2.** To grant. **3.** To agree.

---

car·di·ac

(kär′dē-ăk′) *adj.* Near, of, or relating to the heart.

---

cor·di·al

(kôr′jəl) *adj.* Warm and friendly; gracious. **-cor·dial′i·ty, cor′dial·ness,** *n.* **-cor′dial·ly,** *adv.*

---

cur·sive

(kûr′sĭv) *adj.* Written in flowing strokes where the letters are joined together. **-cur′sive·ly,** *adv.* **-cur′sive·ness,** *n.*

---

cur·so·ry

(kûr′sə-rē) *adj.* Rapid; not thorough; hasty. **-cur′so·ri·ly,** *adv.* **-cur′so·ri·ness,** *n.*

---

gauche

(gōsh) *adj.* Lacking social grace; awkward; tactless. **-gauche′ly,** *adv.* **-gauche′ness,** *n.*

---

na·ive

(nä-ēv′) *adj.* **1.** Lacking in experience or informed judgment. **2.** Childlike; unsophisticated. **-na·ive′ly,** *adv.*

---

non·cha·lant

(nŏn′shə-länt′) *adj.* Showing a lack of interest or enthusiasm; coolly unconcerned.

---

pot·pour·ri

(pō′pŏŏ-rē′) *n., pl.* **-ris. 1.** A mixture or collection of different things. **2.** A mixture of dried flowers and spices used for fragrance.

---

ren·dez·vous

(rän′dā-vōō′, -də-) *n., pl.* **ren·dez·vous. 1.** An agreement to meet at a certain place and time. **2.** The meeting itself.

---

bla·sé

(blä-zā′) *adj.* Uninterested or bored, as from too much of worldly pleasures.

---

cli·ché

(klē-shā′) *n.* An expression or idea that has lost its effect because it has been overused; a trite expression.

---

cli·en·tele

(klī′ən-tel′, klē′ăn-) *n.* Clients and customers as a group.

---

en·trée

(ŏn′trā, ŏn-trā′) *n.* **1.** The right, freedom, or privilege to enter. **2.** The main course or dish of a meal.

---

en·tre·pre·neur

(ŏn′trə-prə-nûr′, -nŏŏr′) *n.* A person who organizes, manages, and assumes the risk of a business or enterprise.

---

du·ra·tion

(dŏŏ-rā′shən, dyŏŏ-) *n.* **1.** The length of time something continues or lasts. **2.** Continuance in time.

---

im·mense

(ĭ-mĕns′) *adj.* **1.** Very large; huge. **2.** Of immeasurable size or extent. **-im·mense′ly,** *adv.* **-im·mense′ness,** *n.*

---

struc·ture

(strŭk′chər) *n.* **1.** The arrangement or interrelation of the parts of a whole. **2.** Something composed of interrelated parts.

---

the·o·ret·i·cal

(thē′ə-rĕt′ĭ-kəl) *adj.* **1.** Not based on fact or experience. **2.** Speculative. **-the·oret′i·cal·ly,** *adv.*

---

vi·cin·i·ty

(vĭ-sĭn′ĭ-tē) *n., pl.* **-ties. 1.** The area around a place; neighborhood. **2.** Nearness; proximity.

---

con·verge

(kən-vûrj′) *v.* **-verged, -verg·ing, -verg·es.** To tend to come together at a place or point. **-con·ver′gence,** *n.* **-con·ver′gent,** *adj.*

---

creep

(krēp) *v.* **crept, creep·ing. 1.** To move with the body close to the ground, as on hands and knees. **2.** To move slowly.

---

cul·mi·nate

(kŭl′mə-nāt′) *v.* **-nat·ed, -nat·ing, -nates. 1.** To reach the highest point or climax. **2.** To come to an end. **-cul′mi·na′tion,** *n.*

---

des·o·late

(dĕs′ə-lĭt, dĕz′-) *adj.* **1.** Devastated. **2.** Uninhabited; deserted. **-des′o·la′tion,** *n.* **-des′o·late·ly,** *adv.*

---

di·verge

(dĭ-vûrj′, dī-) *v.* **-verged, -verg·ing, -verg·es. 1.** To draw apart from a common point. **2.** To differ, as in opinion.

Lesson 9	Lesson 9	Lesson 9	Lesson 9	Lesson 9
discord	discursive	precursor	recourse	recurrent
accord	cardiac	cordial	cursive	cursory

Lesson 8	Lesson 8	Lesson 8	Lesson 8	Lesson 8
gauche	naive	nonchalant	potpourri	rendezvous
blasé	cliché	clientele	entrée	entrepreneur

Lesson 7	Lesson 7	Lesson 7	Lesson 7	Lesson 7
duration	immense	structure	theoretical	vicinity
converge	creep	culminate	desolate	diverge

Lesson 12

ma·nip·u·late
(mə-nĭp′yə-lāt′) v. -lat·ed,
-lat·ing. 1. To work or oper-
ate skillfully with the hands.
2. To manage or control to
one's own advantage.

Lesson 12

ped·es·tal
(pĕd′ĭ-stəl) n. 1. The bottom support of a pillar,
column, statue, etc. 2. A
foundation, support, or
base.

Lesson 12

ped·i·gree
(pĕd′ĭ-grē′) n. 1. A line of
ancestors; lineage. 2. A list of
ancestors; family tree.

Lesson 12

po·di·a·trist
(pə-dī′ə-trĭst) n. A doctor
specializing in the branch of
medicine having to do with
the foot.

Lesson 12

po·di·um
(pō′dē-əm) n., pl. -di·a or
-di·ums. 1. A stand for holding notes of a speaker;
lectern. 2. A raised platform
as for an orchestra conductor.

Lesson 12

coun·ter·mand
(koun′tər-mănd′,
koun′tər-mănd′) v. To cancel
or reverse (an order or command).

Lesson 12

ex·pe·dite
(ĕk′spĭ-dīt′) v. To speed up
the progress of; facilitate.
-ex·pe·dit·er, ex·pe·di·tor, n.

Lesson 12

im·ped·i·ment
(ĭm-pĕd′ə-mənt) n. An ob-
struction; hindrance; obstacle.

Lesson 12

man·date
(măn′dāt) n. An authorization or support given by
voters to their representatives in government. -v. to
require, as by law.

Lesson 12

man·da·to·ry
(măn′də-tôr′ē, -tōr′ē) adj.
1. Required or commanded
by a law, rule, or order. 2. Of
or having a mandate.

Lesson 11

re·ac·tion·ar·y
(rē-ăk′shə-nĕr′ē) adj. Of,
characterized by, or favoring
a return to a former condition, especially in politics.

Lesson 11

se·di·tion
(sĭ-dĭsh′ən) n. Language or
action causing discontent,
resistance, or rebellion
against the government in
power. -se·di′tious, adj.
-se·di′tion·ist, n.

Lesson 11

sov·er·eign
(sŏv′ər-ĭn, sŏv′rĭn) adj. Not
controlled by others; independent. -n. The supreme
ruler. -sov′er·eign·ty, n.

Lesson 11

to·tal·i·tar·i·an
(tō-tăl′ĭ-târ′ē-ən) adj. Of or
relating to a government in
which one political party or
group exercises complete
control.

Lesson 11

u·surp
(yōō-sûrp′, -zûrp′) v. To
take and hold by force and
without legal right or authority. -u·surp′er, n.

Lesson 11

au·ton·o·my
(ô-tŏn′ə-mē) n., pl. -mies.
The state or condition of
being free from outside
control; self-governance.
-au·ton′o·mous, adj.

Lesson 11

bu·reauc·ra·cy
(byoo-rŏk′rə-sē) n. The
administration of govern-
ment and officials following
an inflexible routine.
-bu′reau·crat′ic, adj.

Lesson 11

cod·i·fy
(kŏd′ĭ-fī′, kō′də-) v. -fied,
-fy·ing, -fies. To arrange
systematically.
-cod′i·fi·ca·tion, n.
-cod′i·fi·er, n.

Lesson 11

des·pot
(dĕs′pət) n. A ruler with
unlimited and absolute
power and authority.
-des·pot′ic, adj.
-des·pot′i·cal·ly, adv.

Lesson 11

im·pe·ri·ous
(ĭm-pîr′ē-əs) adj. Over-
bearing; domineering; arrogant. -im·pe′ri·ous·ly, adv.
-im·pe′ri·ous·ness, n.

Lesson 10

ro·bust
(rō-bŭst′, rō′bŭst′) adj.
1. Strong and healthy; vigorous. 2. Requiring strength or
stamina. -ro·bust′ly, adv.
-ro·bust′ness, n.

Lesson 10

ruth·less
(rōōth′lĭs) adj. Without
mercy, pity, or compassion.
-ruth′less·ly, adv.
-ruth′less·ness, n.

Lesson 10

syn·the·sis
(sĭn′thĭ-sĭs) n., pl. -ses
(-sēz′). The combining of
separate parts or elements to
form a whole.

Lesson 10

tra·verse
(trə-vûrs′, trăv′ərs) v.
-versed, -vers·ing, -vers·es.
1. To pass over, across, or
through. 2. To cross and
recross.

Lesson 10

val·i·date
(văl′ĭ-dāt′) v. -dat·ed,
-dat·ing, -dates. 1. To prove
to be true or correct; confirm. 2. To make legally
valid. -val·i·da′tion, n.

Lesson 10

ac·cul·tur·ate
(ə-kŭl′chə-rāt′) v. To adapt
or adjust to the cultural traits
or patterns of another group
as a result of conditioning.
-ac·cul′tur·a′tion, n.

Lesson 10

do·min·ion
(də-mĭn′yən) n. 1. Supreme
authority; rule or power to
rule. 2. A country or terri-
tory controlled by a particular ruler.

Lesson 10

in·dig·e·nous
(ĭn-dĭj′ə-nəs) adj.
Originating in or growing
naturally in a particular re-
gion or country; native.
-in·dig′e·nous·ly, adv.

Lesson 10

plain·tive
(plān′tĭv) adj. Expressing
sorrow or melancholy;
mournful; sad. -plain′tive·ly,
adv. -plain′tive·ness, n.

Lesson 10

quell
(kwĕl) v. 1. To crush; sup-
press. 2. To quiet; pacify.

Lesson 12	Lesson 12	Lesson 11	Lesson 11	Lesson 10
manipulate	countermand	reactionary	autonomy	robust
pedestal	expedite	sedition	bureaucracy	dominion
pedigree	impediment	sovereign	codify	ruthless
podiatrist	mandate	totalitarian	despot	synthesis
podium	mandatory	usurp	imperious	indigenous

Lesson 11	Lesson 10	Lesson 10	Lesson 10
	validate	traverse	acculturate
			plaintive
		synthesis	quell

manipulate — Lesson 12
countermand — Lesson 12
reactionary — Lesson 11
autonomy — Lesson 11
robust — Lesson 10
acculturate — Lesson 10

pedestal — Lesson 12
expedite — Lesson 12
sedition — Lesson 11
bureaucracy — Lesson 11
dominion — Lesson 10

pedigree — Lesson 12
impediment — Lesson 12
sovereign — Lesson 11
codify — Lesson 11
ruthless — Lesson 10
indigenous — Lesson 10

podiatrist — Lesson 12
mandate — Lesson 12
totalitarian — Lesson 11
despot — Lesson 11
synthesis — Lesson 10
plaintive — Lesson 10

podium — Lesson 12
mandatory — Lesson 12
usurp — Lesson 11
imperious — Lesson 11
validate — Lesson 10
quell — Lesson 10

traverse — Lesson 10

Lesson 15

mal·aise
(mă-lāz′, -lĕz′) *n.* A vague feeling of physical discomfort or unease.

ma·lev·o·lence
(mə-lĕv′ə-ləns) *n.* The desire for evil or harm to happen to others; spitefulness.

ma·li·cious
(mə-lĭsh′əs) *adj.* Showing or having the desire to harm, injure, or cause pain to another; spiteful.

ma·lign
(mə-līn′) *v.* To tell evil or harmful lies about. *-adj.* Evil; harmful.

ma·lig·nant
(mə-lĭg′nənt) *adj.* 1. Likely to spread through the body and cause death. 2. Very harmful or evil. **-ma·lig′nant·ly,** *adv.*

Lesson 15

ben·e·dic·tion
(bĕn′ĭ-dĭk′shən) *n.* 1. A blessing. 2. An invocation of a blessing, especially at the end of a religious service.

ben·e·factor
(bĕn′ə-făk′tər) *n.* One who gives help, especially financial aid; patron.

be·nev·o·lent
(bə-nĕv′ə-lənt) *adj.* Doing or wanting to do good; kindly. **-be·nev′o·lent·ly,** *adv.*

be·nign
(bĭ-nīn′) *adj.* 1. Having a kindly disposition. 2. Favorable; beneficial. 3. Not dangerous to health; not malignant.

mal·a·dy
(măl′ə-dē) *n., pl.* **-dies.** 1. A disease or illness. 2. Any unwholesome condition.

Lesson 14

in·dem·ni·fy
(ĭn-dĕm′nə-fī) *v.* **-fied, -fy·ing, -fies.** To insure against future loss, damage, or expense. **-in·dem′ni·fi·ca′tion,** *n.*

liq·ui·date
(lĭk′wĭ-dāt′) *v.* **-dat·ed, -dat·ing, -dates.** 1. To pay off or settle (a debt). 2. To convert (assets) to cash. **-liq′ui·da′tion,** *n.*

lu·cra·tive
(loo′krə-tĭv) *adj.* Producing money or wealth; profitable. **-lu′cra·tive·ly,** *adv.*

pe·cu·ni·ar·y
(pĭ-kyoo′nē-ĕr′ē) *adj.* Of, consisting of, or relating to money.

usu·ry
(yoo′zhə-rē) *n., pl.* **-ries.** 1. The practice of lending money at an excessive interest rate. 2. An excessive interest rate.

Lesson 14

ac·crue
(ə-kroo′) *v.* **-crued, -cru·ing, -crues.** 1. To grow in amount over time. 2. To result as from natural growth or addition.

au·dit
(ô′dĭt) *v.* To examine financial accounts and records to determine if they are correct. *-n.* A formal examination of financial records.

cap·i·tal
(kăp′ĭ-tl) *n.* 1. Wealth in any form used or capable of being used to produce more wealth. 2. The total amount of money or property owned.

car·tel
(kär-tĕl′) *n.* A group of companies or businesses formed to control production, prices, and marketing of its members' goods.

col·lat·er·al
(kə-lăt′ər-əl) *n.* Property given as security for the repayment of a loan. **-col·lat′er·al·ly,** *adv.*

Lesson 13

frus·tra·tion
(frŭ-strā′shən) *n.* A feeling of disappointment resulting from being unable to accomplish something or from a defeat. **-frus′trate,** *v.*

gal·va·nize
(găl′və-nīz′) *v.* **-nized, -niz·ing, -niz·es.** To rouse suddenly to awareness or action; startle; excite. **-gal′va·niza′tion,** *n.*

im·meas·ur·a·ble
(ĭ-mĕzh′ər-ə-bəl) *adj.* That which cannot be measured; boundless; vast. **-im·meas′ur·a·bil′i·ty,** *n.* **-im·meas′ur·a·bly,** *adv.*

in·de·fat·i·ga·ble
(ĭn′dĭ-făt′ĭ-gə-bəl) *adj.* Incapable of being tired out; tireless. **-in·de·fat′i·ga·bil′i·ty,** *n.* **-in·de·fat′i·ga·bly,** *adv.*

re·nown
(rĭ-noun′) *n.* Widespread fame. **-re·nowned′,** *adj.*

Lesson 13

a·bridge
(ə-brĭj′) *v.* **a·bridged, a·bridg·ing, a·bridg·es.** 1. To restrict; curtail. 2. To shorten; condense. **-a·bridg′ment,** *n.*

char·ac·ter
(kăr′ək-tər) *n.* 1. All the good and bad qualities of a person that constitute his or her moral nature. 2. Moral strength; integrity.

cha·ris·mat·ic
(kăr′ĭz-măt′ĭk) *adj.* Possessing personal magnetism or charm that attracts many followers. **-cha·ris′ma,** *n.*

creed
(krēd) *n.* 1. A statement of belief, principles, or opinions. 2. A formal statement of religious belief.

e·ven·tu·al
(ĭ-vĕn′choo-əl) *adj.* Happening as a result of events that go before; ultimate; final. **-even′tu·al·ly,** *adv.*

Lesson 15 malignant	Lesson 15 malign	Lesson 15 malicious	Lesson 15 malevolence	Lesson 15 malaise
Lesson 15 malady	Lesson 15 benign	Lesson 15 benevolent	Lesson 15 benefactor	Lesson 15 benediction
Lesson 14 usury	Lesson 14 pecuniary	Lesson 14 lucrative	Lesson 14 liquidate	Lesson 14 indemnify
Lesson 14 collateral	Lesson 14 cartel	Lesson 14 capital	Lesson 14 audit	Lesson 14 accrue
Lesson 13 renown	Lesson 13 indefatigable	Lesson 13 immeasurable	Lesson 13 galvanize	Lesson 13 frustration
Lesson 13 eventual	Lesson 13 creed	Lesson 13 charismatic	Lesson 13 character	Lesson 13 abridge

Lesson 18	Lesson 18	Lesson 18	Lesson 18	Lesson 18
pa·thet·ic (pə-thĕt′ĭk) *adj.* Arousing pity or sadness combined with either sympathy or contempt.	**pa·thol·o·gy** (pă-thŏl′ə-jē) *n.*, *pl.* **-gies.** The branch of medicine that deals with the nature, cause, and development of disease.	**pa·thos** (pā′thŏs, -thôs) *n.* The quality in something that evokes a feeling of pity, sadness, or compassion.	**psy·cho·path** (sī′kə-păth′) *n.* A person having a serious mental disorder characterized by amoral or antisocial behavior.	**xen·o·pho·bi·a** (zĕn′ə-fō′bē-ə) *n.* Fear or hatred of strangers or anything strange or foreign. **-xen′o·pho′bic,** *adj.*

Lesson 18	Lesson 18	Lesson 18	Lesson 18	Lesson 18
ac·ro·pho·bi·a (ăk′rə-fō′bē-ə) *n.* An abnormal fear of being in high places.	**ap·a·thy** (ăp′ə-thē) *n.* **1.** Lack of interest or concern; indifference. **2.** Lack of emotion.	**claus·tro·pho·bi·a** (klô′strə-fō′bē-ə) *n.* An abnormal fear of being in an enclosed, narrow, or small place.	**em·pa·thy** (ĕm′pə-thē) *n.* A sharing and understanding of another's feelings, situation, or state of mind.	**hy·dro·pho·bi·a** (hī′drə-fō′bē-ə) *n.* **1.** An abnormal fear of water. **2.** Rabies.

Lesson 17	Lesson 17	Lesson 17	Lesson 17	Lesson 17
con·tin·u·ous (kən-tĭn′yōō-əs) *adj.* Going on without interruption; unbroken. **-con·tin′u·ous·ly,** *adv.* **-con·tin′u·ous·ness,** *n.*	**dis·in·ter·est·ed** (dĭs-ĭn′trĭ-stĭd, -ĭn′tə-rĕs′tĭd) *adj.* Not influenced by a personal interest; impartial. **-dis·in′ter·est·ed·ly,** *adv.* **-dis·in′ter·est·ed·ness,** *n.*	**un·in·ter·est·ed** (ŭn-ĭn′trĭ-stĭd, -tar-ĭ-stĭd, -tə-rĕs′tĭd) *adj.* Not interested; indifferent. **-un·in′ter·est·ed·ly,** *adv.* **-un·in′ter·est·ed·ness,** *n.*	**im·ply** (ĭm-plī′) *v.* **-plied, -ply·ing, -plies.** To express or suggest indirectly; hint.	**in·fer** (ĭn-fûr′) *v.* **-ferred, -fer·ring, -fers.** To conclude from facts or observations.

Lesson 17	Lesson 17	Lesson 17	Lesson 17	Lesson 17
af·fect (ə-fĕkt′) *v.* **1.** To produce an effect in; influence. **2.** To move the emotions of. *-n.* (ăf′-ĕkt′) An emotion or feeling.	**ef·fect** (ĭ-fĕkt′) *n.* Anything brought about by a cause or agent; result. *-v.* To bring about or cause.	**a·venge** (ə-vĕnj′) *v.* **avenged, aveng·es, aveng·es. 1.** To get revenge for. **2.** To take vengeance on behalf of. **-aveng′er,** *n.*	**re·venge** (rĭ-vĕnj′) *n.* A desire to inflict, or the act of inflicting, harm, injury, or punishment in return for a wrong.	**con·tin·u·al** (kən-tĭn′yōō-əl) *adj.* Repeated frequently. **con·tin′u·al·ly,** *adv.*

Lesson 16	Lesson 16	Lesson 16	Lesson 16	Lesson 16
in·duce (ĭn-dōōs′, -dyōōs′) *v.* **-duced, -duc·ing, -duc·es. 1.** To lead to an action; persuade. **2.** To bring about; cause. **-in·duc′i·ble,** *adj.*	**in·gre·di·ent** (ĭn-grē′dē-ənt) *n.* Any one of the elements of a mixture.	**in·her·ent** (ĭn-hîr′ənt, -hĕr′-) *adj.* Existing in someone or something as a permanent or basic characteristic. **-in·her′ent·ly,** *adv.*	**prev·a·lent** (prĕv′ə-lənt) *adj.* Widely, commonly, or generally happening, existing, accepted, or practiced. **-prev′a·lent·ly,** *adv.*	**sur·pass** (sər-păs′) *v.* **1.** To go beyond; excel. **2.** Exceed. **-sur·pass′a·ble,** *adj.* **-sur·pass′ing·ly,** *adv.*

Lesson 16	Lesson 16	Lesson 16	Lesson 16	Lesson 16
at·mo·sphere (ăt′mə-sfîr′) *n.* The gaseous mass surrounding the earth or any celestial body.	**col·lide** (kə-līd′) *v.* **1.** To come together with forceful impact; crash. **2.** To conflict; clash.	**de·pict** (dĭ-pĭkt′) *v.* **1.** To represent by drawing or painting; portray. **2.** To picture in words; describe. **-de·pic′tion,** *n.*	**ex·hi·bi·tion** (ĕk′sə-bĭsh′ən) *n.* **1.** The act of showing publicly. **2.** A public display.	**im·pres·sive** (ĭm-prĕs′ĭv) *adj.* Producing attention, wonder, respect, or admiration. **-im·pres′sive·ly,** *adv.* **-im·pres′sive·ness,** *n.*

Lesson 18 pathetic	Lesson 18 pathology	Lesson 18 pathos	Lesson 18 psychopath
Lesson 18 xenophobia	Lesson 18 hydrophobia	Lesson 18 empathy	Lesson 18 claustrophobia
Lesson 18 acrophobia	Lesson 18 apathy	Lesson 17 continuous	Lesson 17 uninterested
Lesson 17 infer	Lesson 17 imply	Lesson 17 disinterested	Lesson 17 affect
Lesson 17 effect	Lesson 17 avenge	Lesson 17 revenge	Lesson 17 continual
Lesson 16 induce	Lesson 16 ingredient	Lesson 16 inherent	Lesson 16 prevalent
Lesson 16 surpass	Lesson 16 atmosphere	Lesson 16 collide	Lesson 16 depict
Lesson 16 exhibition	Lesson 16 impressive		

Lesson 21

non·de·script
(nŏn'dĭ-skrĭpt') *adj.* Having no interesting or distinctive qualities or characteristics.

Lesson 21

post·script
(pōst'skrĭpt', pōs'skrĭpt') *n. Abbr.* **P.S., p.s., PS.** A note added to the end of a letter after the writer's signature.

Lesson 21

pro·scribe
(prō-skrīb') *v.* **-scribed, -scrib·ing, -scribes. 1.** To forbid. **2.** To condemn. **3.** To banish. **-proscrib'er**, *n.*

Lesson 21

pro·tract
(prō-trăkt', prə-) *v.* To lengthen or draw out; prolong. **-pro·tract'ed·ly,** *adv.* **-pro·tract'ed·ness,** *n.* **-pro·trac'tive,** *adj.*

Lesson 21

scrip·ture
(skrĭp'chər) *n.* A sacred or religious writing or book.

Lesson 21

as·cribe
(ə-skrīb') *v.* **-cribed, -crib·ing, -cribes. 1.** To assign to a particular cause, source, or origin. **2.** To regard as belonging to.

Lesson 21

con·script
(kən-skrĭpt') *v.* To enroll by law to serve in the armed forces; draft. *-n.* (kŏn'skrĭpt) Draftee.

Lesson 21

de·tract
(dĭ-trăkt') *v.* To take away value, quality, or importance; divert. **-de·trac'tion,** *n.*

Lesson 21

ex·tract
(ĭk-străkt') *v.* **1.** To draw or pull out with effort. **2.** To obtain or separate by pressing, distilling, etc. **-ex·trac'tion,** *n.*

Lesson 21

in·trac·ta·ble
(ĭn-trăk'tə-bəl) *adj.* Hard to manage; stubborn; unruly. **-in·trac'ta·bil'i·ty,** *n.* **-in·trac'ta·bly,** *adv.*

Lesson 20

met·a·phor
(mĕt'ə-fôr', -fər) *n.* A figure of speech in which one thing is compared to another to suggest a similarity.

Lesson 20

par·o·dy
(păr'ə-dē) *n., pl.* **-dies.** A humorous or satirical literary or musical imitation of a serious work.

Lesson 20

pa·tois
(păt'wä, pă-twä') *n., pl.* **pat·ois.** A regional dialect of a language, especially one other than the standard or literary dialect.

Lesson 20

sol·e·cism
(sŏl'ĭ-sĭz'əm, sō'lĭ-) *n.* An error in grammar or standard usage of language.

Lesson 20

so·lil·o·quy
(sə-lĭl'ə-kwē) *n., pl.* **-quies. 1.** The act of talking to oneself. **2.** Lines in a play that a character says aloud to himself or herself.

Lesson 20

al·le·go·ry
(ăl'ĭ-gôr'ē, -gōr'ē) *n., pl.* **-ries.** A story in which the characters represent moral principles or ideas.

Lesson 20

al·lu·sion
(ə-lōō'zhən) *n.* An indirect reference made to something.

Lesson 20

con·no·ta·tion
(kŏn'ə-tā'shən) *n.* A meaning or idea that is associated with a word in addition to its literal meaning.

Lesson 20

id·i·om
(ĭd'ē-əm) *n.* A phrase or expression whose meaning is different from the literal meaning of its individual words.

Lesson 20

jar·gon
(jär'gən) *n.* The specialized vocabulary used by those in a particular profession or way of life.

Lesson 19

pro·found
(prə-found', prō-) *adj.* **1.** Showing great understanding. **2.** Deeply felt. **3.** Significant; far-reaching. **-pro·found'ly,** *adv.*

Lesson 19

pro·sa·ic
(prō-zā'ĭk) *adj.* **1.** Commonplace; dull. **2.** Matter-of-fact. **-pro·sa'i·cal·ly,** *adv.* **-pro·sa'ic·ness,** *n.*

Lesson 19

re·lent·less
(rĭ-lĕnt'lĭs) *adj.* **1.** Steady and persistent. **2.** Harsh; pitiless. **-re·lent'less·ly,** *adv.* **-re·lent'less·ness,** *n.*

Lesson 19

syn·tax
(sĭn'tăks') *n.* The manner in which words are arranged to form sentences.

Lesson 19

ten·et
(tĕn'ĭt) *n.* A principle, doctrine, or belief held as truth by a person or group.

Lesson 19

fa·cil·i·tate
(fə-sĭl'ĭ-tāt') *v.* **-tat·ed, -tat·ing, -tates.** To make easy or easier; help. **-fa·cil'i·ta'tive,** *adj.* **-fa·cil'i·ta'tor,** *n.*

Lesson 19

fos·ter
(fô'stər, fŏ'stər) *v.* **1.** To help the growth and development of; promote. **2.** To bring up; rear.

Lesson 19

legion
(lē'jən) *n.* A large number; multitude.

Lesson 19

nas·cent
(năs'ənt, nā'sənt) *adj.* Coming into being; beginning to develop. **-nas'cen·cy,** *n.*

Lesson 19

nov·ice
(nŏv'ĭs) *n.* A person new to an activity; beginner.

Lesson 21 nondescript	Lesson 21 ascribe	Lesson 20 metaphor	Lesson 20 allegory	Lesson 19 profound	Lesson 19 facilitate
Lesson 21 postscript	Lesson 21 conscript	Lesson 20 parody	Lesson 20 allusion	Lesson 19 prosaic	Lesson 19 foster
Lesson 21 proscribe	Lesson 21 detract	Lesson 20 patois	Lesson 20 connotation	Lesson 19 relentless	Lesson 19 legion
Lesson 21 protract	Lesson 21 extract	Lesson 20 solecism	Lesson 20 idiom	Lesson 19 syntax	Lesson 19 nascent
Lesson 21 scripture	Lesson 21 intractable	Lesson 20 soliloquy	Lesson 20 jargon	Lesson 19 tenet	Lesson 19 novice

Lesson 24

in·tact (ĭn-tăkt') *adj.* Not damaged; unimpaired; untouched; uninjured. **-in·tact'ly,** *adv.* **-in·tact'ness,** *n.*

sub·jec·tive (səb-jĕk'tĭv) *adj.* Of or coming from the individual's own mind, based on the person's own feelings, thoughts, or experiences.

tact (tăkt) *n.* The skill in dealing with people or delicate situations without offending.

tan·gent (tăn'jənt) *adj.* In contact at a single point; touching.

tan·gi·ble (tăn'jə-bəl) *adj.* 1. Capable of being touched. 2. Capable of being treated as definite or fact; real; concrete.

Lesson 24

ab·ject (ăb'jĕkt, ăb-jĕkt') *adj.* 1. Miserable; wretched. 2. Contemptible; despicable. **-ab·ject'ly,** *adv.* **-ab·ject'ness,** *n.*

ad·ja·cent (ə-jā'sənt) *adj.* Lying near; adjoining. **-adja·cent·ly,** *adv.*

con·jec·ture (kən-jĕk'chər) *n.* 1. Judgment based on insufficient or incomplete evidence. 2. A guess.

con·tig·u·ous (kən-tĭg'yoo-əs) *adj.* 1. In contact; touching. 2. Near; close. **-con·tig'u·ousness,** *n.*

con·tin·gent (kən-tĭn'jənt) *adj.* 1. Dependent on uncertain conditions or events. 2. Possible. **-con·tin'gen·cy,** *n.*

Lesson 23

er·rant (ĕr'ənt) *adj.* 1. Roving in search of adventure; wandering. 2. Straying from correct behavior; erring.

er·rat·ic (ĭ-răt'ĭk) *adj.* 1. Having no regular course; wandering. 2. Irregular; unpredictable. **-errat'i·caly,** *adv.*

id·i·o·syn·crat·ic (ĭd'ē-ō-sĭn-krăt'ĭk) *adj.* Having a peculiar or distinguishing mannerism or characteristic. **-id'i·osyn'cra·sy,** *n.*

in·con·gru·ous (ĭn-kŏng'groo-əs) *adj.* Lacking harmony; incompatible; unsuitable. **-in·con'gru·ous·ly,** *adv.*

out·land·ish (out-lăn'dĭsh) *adj.* Strange; odd; peculiar. **-out·land'ish·ly,** *adv.* **-out·land'ish·ness,** *n.*

Lesson 23

ab·er·rant (ă-bĕr'ənt) *adj.* Deviating from what is usual, normal, or correct. **-aber'rance, aber'ran·cy,** *n.* **-aber'rantly,** *adv.*

a·nom·a·ly (ə-nŏm'ə-lē) *n., pl.* **-lies.** Something different from the usual or normal; abnormality.

bi·zarre (bĭ-zär') *adj.* Odd or strange in appearance or manner; grotesque. **-bizarre'ly,** *adv.* **-bizarre'ness,** *n.*

de·vi·ate (dē've-āt') *v.* **-at·ed, -at·ing, -ates.** 1. To turn aside from a course, standard, or subject. 2. To depart from a norm.

ec·cen·tric·i·ty (ĕk'sĕn-trĭs'ĭ-tē) *n., pl.* **-ties.** An act or trait that differs from the usual; peculiarity.

Lesson 22

mil·i·tant (mĭl'ĭ-tənt) *adj.* 1. Aggressive or vigorously active in support of a cause. 2. Fighting. *-n.* One who acts aggressively.

pre·em·i·nent (prē-ĕm'ə-nənt) *adj.* Superior to or above others; outstanding. **-pre·em'inence,** *n.* **-pre·em'i·nently,** *adv.*

rel·e·gate (rĕl'ĭ-gāt') *v.* **-gat·ed, -gat·ing, -gates.** To banish. To assign to an inferior position or place. **-rel·ega'tion,** *n.*

sanc·tion (săngk'shən) *n.* Authorization; official approval. *-v.* To give authorization or official approval to.

se·rene (sə-rēn') *adj.* Undisturbed; peaceful; calm. **-se·rene'ly,** *adv.* **-se·ren'i·ty,** *n.*

Lesson 22

an·nals (ăn'əlz) *pl.n.* 1. Historical records; history. 2. A written record of chronological events.

con·found (kən-found', kŏn-) *v.* To confuse or perplex; bewilder. **-con·found'er,** *n.* **-con·found'edly,** *adv.*

feis·ty (fī'stē) *adj.* **-i·er, -i·est.** 1. Ill-tempered; touchy; quarrelsome. 2. Spirited; frisky. **-feist'i·ness,** *n.*

hale (hāl) *adj.* Healthy; vigorous; robust. **-hale'ness,** *n.*

lon·gev·i·ty (lŏn-jĕv'ĭ-tē, lôn-) *n., pl.* **-ties.** Long life.

Lesson 24 — intact	Lesson 24 — subjective	Lesson 24 — tact	Lesson 24 — tangent	Lesson 24 — tangible
Lesson 24 — abject	Lesson 24 — adjacent	Lesson 24 — conjecture	Lesson 24 — contiguous	Lesson 24 — contingent
Lesson 23 — errant	Lesson 23 — erratic	Lesson 23 — idiosyncratic	Lesson 23 — incongruous	Lesson 23 — outlandish
Lesson 23 — aberrant	Lesson 23 — anomaly	Lesson 23 — bizarre	Lesson 23 — deviate	Lesson 23 — eccentricity
Lesson 22 — militant	Lesson 22 — preeminent	Lesson 22 — relegate	Lesson 22 — sanction	Lesson 22 — serene
Lesson 22 — annals	Lesson 22 — confound	Lesson 22 — feisty	Lesson 22 — hale	Lesson 22 — longevity

Lesson 27

port·fo·li·o

(pôrt-fō′lē-ō, pōrt-) *n., pl.* **-os. 1.** A portable case for carrying loose papers, etc. **2.** A representative collection of a person's work.

Lesson 27

port·ly

(pôrt′lē, pōrt′-) *adj.* **-li·er, -li·est.** Large and heavy; stout; obese. **-port′li·ness,** *n.*

Lesson 27

pur·port

(pər-pôrt′, -pōrt′) *v.* **1.** To profess or claim, often falsely. **2.** To mean; intend. *-n.* Meaning.

Lesson 27

rap·port

(ră-pôr′, -pōr′, ră-) *n.* A close, harmonious relationship.

Lesson 27

spor·tive

(spôr′tĭv, spōr′-) *adj.* **1.** Playful; frolicsome. **2.** Interested in sports. **-spor′tive·ly,** *adv.* **-spor′tive·ness,** *n.*

Lesson 27

com·port

(kəm-pôrt′, -pōrt′) *v.* To behave or conduct (oneself) in a specified manner. **-com·port′ment,** *n.*

Lesson 27

de·port·ment

(dĭ-pôrt′mənt, -pōrt′-) *n.* The manner in which a person behaves or acts; conduct.

Lesson 27

op·por·tune

(ŏp′ər-to͞on′, -tyo͞on′) *adj.* **1.** Suitable for a particular purpose. **2.** Happening at the right time; well-timed; timely. **-op′por·tune′ly,** *adv.*

Lesson 27

port·a·ble

(pôr′tə-bəl, pōr′-) *adj.* Able to be carried or moved easily. **-port·a·bil′i·ty,** *n.* **-port′a·bly,** *adv.*

Lesson 27

port·age

(pôr′tĭj, pōr′-, pôr-täzh′) *n.* The carrying of boats or supplies from one navigable body of water to another.

Lesson 26

in·sa·tia·ble

(ĭn-sā′shə-bəl, -shē-ə-) *adj.* Not able to be satisfied. **-in·sa′tia·bly,** *adv.*

Lesson 26

i·o·ta

(ī-ō′tə) *n.* A very small amount.

Lesson 26

pal·try

(pôl′trē) *adj.* **-tri·er, -tri·est.** Lacking in value; worthless. **-pal′tri·ly,** *adv.* **-pal′tri·ness,** *n.*

Lesson 26

pit·tance

(pĭt′ns) *n.* **1.** A small amount of money. **2.** A small amount.

Lesson 26

pleth·o·ra

(plĕth′ər-ə) *n.* An overabundance; too much; excess.

Lesson 26

ac·cre·tion

(ə-krē′shən) *n.* Increase in size by gradual outside addition or natural growth.

Lesson 26

ap·pre·cia·ble

(ə-prē′shə-bəl) *adj.* Enough to be measured or noticed; perceptible. **-ap·pre′cia·bly,** *adv.*

Lesson 26

co·pi·ous

(kō′pē-əs) *adj.* Abundant; plentiful. **-co′pi·ous·ly,** *adv.* **-co′pi·ous·ness,** *n.*

Lesson 26

fath·om·less

(făth′əm-lĭs) *adj.* **1.** Too deep to be measured. **2.** Difficult to understand. **-fath′om·less·ly,** *adv.* **-fath′om·less·ness,** *n.*

Lesson 26

fi·nite

(fī′nīt′) *adj.* Having measurable limits. **-fi′nite·ly,** *adv.* **-fi′nite′ness,** *n.*

Lesson 25

kin·dred

(kĭn′drĭd) *adj.* Related; like; similar.

Lesson 25

min·i·mal

(mĭn′ə-məl) *adj.* Smallest or least possible. **-min′i·mal·ly,** *adv.*

Lesson 25

spawn

(spôn) *v.* To bring forth; produce.

Lesson 25

spe·cif·ic

(spĭ-sĭf′ĭk) *adj.* Definite; explicit; precise. **-spe·cif′i·cal·ly,** *adv.* **-spec′i·fic′i·ty,** *n.*

Lesson 25

sus·tain

(sə-stān′) *v.* **1.** To keep in effect; maintain. **2.** Support. **-sus·tain′a·ble,** *adj.* **-sus·tain′er,** *n.*

Lesson 25

ab·nor·mal

(ăb-nôr′məl) *adj.* Not usual, average, or normal; unusual. **-ab·nor′mal·ly,** *adv.* **-ab′nor·mal′i·ty,** *n.*

Lesson 25

cat·a·stroph·ic

(kăt′ə-strŏf′ĭk) *adj.* Of or relating to a great and sudden disaster. **-ca·tas′tro·phe,** *n.*

Lesson 25

con·spir·a·cy

(kən-spîr′ə-sē) *n., pl.* **-cies.** A secret plan to perform together an evil or wrongful act; plot.

Lesson 25

gen·er·ate

(jĕn′ə-rāt′) *v.* **-at·ed, -at·ing, -ates.** To bring into existence.

Lesson 25

in·ter·vene

(ĭn′tər-vēn′) *v.* **-vened, -ven·ing, -venes. 1.** To come between to alter, affect, or prevent an action. **2.** To come between two things. **-in′ter·ven′tion,** *n.*

Lesson 27	portfolio	Lesson 27	comport
Lesson 27	portly	Lesson 27	deportment
Lesson 27	purport	Lesson 27	opportune
Lesson 27	rapport	Lesson 27	portable
Lesson 27	sportive	Lesson 27	portage
Lesson 26	insatiable	Lesson 26	accretion
Lesson 26	iota	Lesson 26	appreciable
Lesson 26	paltry	Lesson 26	copious
Lesson 26	pittance	Lesson 26	fathomless
Lesson 26	plethora	Lesson 26	finite
Lesson 25	kindred	Lesson 25	abnormal
Lesson 25	minimal	Lesson 25	catastrophic
Lesson 25	spawn	Lesson 25	conspiracy
Lesson 25	specific	Lesson 25	generate
Lesson 25	sustain	Lesson 25	intervene

Lesson 30	Lesson 30	Lesson 30	Lesson 30	Lesson 30
omission	premise	remission	transmit	unremitting
Lesson 30	Lesson 30	Lesson 30	Lesson 30	Lesson 30
emissary	emit	intermittent	manumit	missive
Lesson 29	Lesson 29	Lesson 29	Lesson 29	Lesson 29
extort	felony	incorrigible	pilfer	reprobate
Lesson 29	Lesson 29	Lesson 29	Lesson 29	Lesson 29
charlatan	clemency	culpable	culprit	exonerate
Lesson 28	Lesson 28	Lesson 28	Lesson 28	Lesson 28
ravage	refine	remunerative	scourge	wield
Lesson 28	Lesson 28	Lesson 28	Lesson 28	Lesson 28
aegis	amnesty	ensue	hue	illustrious

im·pos·tor
(ĭm-pŏs′tər) *n.* A person who deceives or cheats others by pretending to be someone else.

jux·ta·po·si·tion
(jŭk′stə-pə-zĭsh′ən) *n.* The placement of things side by side or close together, especially for comparison or contrast.

pro·pound
(prə-pound′) *v.* To put forward for consideration; set forth. **-pro·pound′ er,** *n.*

re·pos·i·to·ry
(rĭ-pŏz′ĭ-tôr′ē, -tōr′ē) *n., pl.* **-ries.** A place where things may be stored or deposited for safekeeping.

sup·po·si·tion
(sŭp′ə-zĭsh′ən) *n.* **1.** An assumption that something is true for the sake of argument. **2.** A belief on uncertain grounds.

com·po·nent
(kəm-pō′nənt) *n.* An essential part, element, or ingredient. *-adj.* Being one of the parts of a whole.

com·pos·ite
(kəm-pŏz′ĭt) *adj.* Made up of separate parts or elements; compound. *-n.* Something that is made up of separate parts.

dis·po·si·tion
(dĭs′pə-zĭsh′ən) *n.* **1.** One's usual way of acting, thinking, or feeling; temperament. **2.** A tendency or inclination.

ex·po·nent
(ĭk-spō′nənt, ĕk′spō′nənt) *n.* **1.** A person who explains or interprets something. **2.** A person who represents, speaks for, or advocates.

ex·pound
(ĭk-spound′) *v.* **1.** To set forth in detail. **2.** To explain in detail. **-ex·pound er,** *n.*

dis·sen·sion
(dĭ-sĕn′shən) *n.* Difference of opinion; disagreement; strife.

os·tra·cize
(ŏs′trə-sīz′) **-cized, -ciz·ing, -ciz·es.** *v.* To banish or exclude from a group. **-os′tra·cism,** *n.*

pug·na·cious
(pŭg-nā′shəs) *adj.* Eager and ready to fight; quarrelsome. **-pug·na′ciously,** *adv.* **-pug·na′ciousness,** **-pug·nac′i·ty,** *n.*

ran·cor
(răng′kər) *n.* Deep or bitter resentment or ill will; hatred. **-ran′cor·ous,** *adj.* **-ran′cor·ously,** *adv.* **-ran′cor·ousness,** *n.*

ret·ri·bu·tion
(rĕt′rə-byōō′shən) *n.* Punishment given or demanded in repayment for evil done.

a·cer·bi·ty
(ə-sûr′bĭ-tē) *n., pl.* **-ties.** Sharpness or bitterness of words, temper, or tone. **-a·cer′bic,** *adj.* **-a·cer′bi·cal·ly,** *adv.*

af·front
(ə-frŭnt′) *v.* To insult deliberately, especially openly. *-n.* A deliberate and open insult.

al·ter·ca·tion
(ôl′tər-kā′shən) *n.* An angry and heated quarrel.

an·tag·o·nism
(ăn-tăg′ə-nĭz′əm) *n.* Strong feeling against; hostility; opposition.

con·ten·tious
(kən-tĕn′shəs) *adj.* Argumentative; quarrelsome. **-con·ten′tiously,** *adv.* **-con·ten′tious·ness,** **-con·ten′tion,** *n.*

le·git·i·mate
(lə-jĭt′ə-mĭt) *adj.* **1.** Lawful. **2.** Logically correct. **3.** Genuine. **-le·git′i·mately,** *adv.* **-le·git′i·mate·ness,** *n.*

sar·to·ri·al
(sär-tôr′ē-əl, -tōr′-) *adj.* **1.** Of tailors or their work. **2.** Of clothing or dress. **-sar·to′ri·al·ly,** *adv.*

staunch
(stônch, stänch) *adj.* **1.** Loyal and steadfast. **2.** Having a strong or solid construction. **-staunch′ly,** *adv.* **-staunch′ness,** *n.*

stra·te·gic
(strə-tē′jĭk) *adj.* Related to a skillful plan intended to achieve a specific goal. **-strat′e·gy,** *n.* **-strate′gi·cal·ly,** *adv.*

ver·sa·tile
(vûr′sə-təl, -tīl′) *adj.* **1.** Capable of doing many things well. **2.** Having many uses. **-ver′sa·tile·ly,** *adv.* **-ver·sa·til′i·ty,** *n.*

com·mod·i·ty
(kə-mŏd′ĭ-tē) *n., pl.* **-ties.** Anything that can be bought and sold; article of trade.

cov·et
(kŭv′ĭt) *v.* To desire ardently (especially something that belongs to another). **-cov′et·a·ble, cov′etous** *adj.* **-cov′etous·ness,** *n.*

ex·trin·sic
(ĭk-strĭn′sĭk, -zĭk) *adj.* **1.** Not essential to the nature of a thing. **2.** Coming from the outside; external. **-ex·trin′si·cally,** *adv.*

gra·tu·i·tous
(grə-tōō′ĭ-təs, tyōō′-) *adj.* **1.** Given without charge; free. **2.** Without justification; uncalled for. **-gra·tu′i·tously,** *adv.* **-gra·tu′i·tous·ness,** *n.*

hal·lowed
(hăl′ōd) *adj.* **1.** Holy; sanctified. **2.** Highly respected.

Lesson 33 impostor	Lesson 33 component	Lesson 32 dissension	Lesson 32 acerbity	Lesson 31 legitimate	Lesson 31 commodity
Lesson 33 juxtaposition	Lesson 33 composite	Lesson 32 ostracize	Lesson 32 affront	Lesson 31 sartorial	Lesson 31 covet
Lesson 33 propound	Lesson 33 disposition	Lesson 32 pugnacious	Lesson 32 altercation	Lesson 31 staunch	Lesson 31 extrinsic
Lesson 33 repository	Lesson 33 exponent	Lesson 32 rancor	Lesson 32 antagonism	Lesson 31 strategic	Lesson 31 gratuitous
Lesson 33 supposition	Lesson 33 expound	Lesson 32 retribution	Lesson 32 contentious	Lesson 31 versatile	Lesson 31 hallowed

Lesson 34

anx·ie·ty (ăng-zī′ĭ-tē) *n., pl.* **-ties. 1.** Worry or feeling of uneasiness about what may happen. **2.** A cause of this feeling.

ap·pall (ə-pôl′) *v.* To dismay or horrify; shock.

ap·pre·ci·ate (ə-prē′shē-āt′) *v.* **-at·ed, -at·ing, -ates. 1.** To recognize the quality, value, or significance of. **2.** To be aware of or sensitive to.

con·verse (kŏn′vûrs′) *n.* Something opposite or reversed; the opposite. **-con·verse′ly,** *adv.*

e·co·nom·ic (ĕk′ə-nŏm′ĭk, ē′kə-) *adj.* Of or relating to financial matters or concerns.

in·ter·de·pend·ence (ĭn′tər-dĭ-pĕn′dəns) *n.* A state of mutual reliance on the aid of each other. **-in′ter·de·pend′ent,** *adj.*

in·tri·cate (ĭn′trĭ-kĭt) *adj.* **1.** Having elaborate detail; complicated. **2.** Hard to understand. **-in′tri·cate·ly,** *adv.* **-in′tri·ca·cy,** *n.*

myr·i·ad (mĭr′ē-əd) *adj.* Too many to count; countless. *n.* A great number.

nur·ture (nûr′chər) *v.* **1.** To feed; nourish. **2.** To educate; foster. *-n.* Something that nourishes. **-nur′tur·er,** *n.*

se·ren·i·ty (sə-rĕn′ĭ-tē) *n.* The state or quality of being calm; tranquility; peacefulness.

Lesson 35

bra·zen (brā′zən) *adj.* **1.** Shameless; impudent. **2.** Made of brass. **-bra′zen·ly,** *adv.* **-bra′zen·ness,** *n.*

dex·ter·ous (dĕk′stər-əs, -strəs) *adj.* Skillful in the use of the hands, body, or mind. **-dex′ter·ous·ly,** *adv.* **-dex′ter·ous·ness,** *n.*

in·cur·sion (ĭn-kûr′zhən, -shən) *n.* A hostile invasion or raid.

pal·pi·tate (păl′pĭ-tāt′) *v.* **-tat·ed, -tat·ing, -tates. 1.** To beat rapidly. **2.** To quiver or tremble. **-pal′pi·tat′ing·ly,** *adv.*

re·doubt·a·ble (rĭ-dou′tə-bəl) *adj.* **1.** Formidable; awesome. **2.** Deserving of respect. **-re·doubt′a·bly,** *adv.*

res·o·lute (rĕz′ə-lōot′) *adj.* Determined; firm. **-res′o·lute′ly,** *adv.* **-res′o·lute′ness,** *n.*

sal·ly (săl′ē) *v.* **-lied, -ly·ing, -lies. 1.** To rush out suddenly. **2.** To go out quickly.

stal·wart (stôl′wərt) *adj.* **1.** Firm and steadfast; unwavering. **2.** Strong. *-n.* A person who is firm, steadfast, or strong. **-stal′wart·ly,** *adv.* **-stal′wart·ness,** *n.*

stam·i·na (stăm′ə-nə) *n.* Resistance to illness, fatigue, or hardship; endurance.

ve·he·ment (vē′ə-mənt) *adj.* Characterized by intense or strong feeling or conviction; passionate. **-ve′he·mence,** *n.* **-ve′he·ment·ly,** *adv.*

Lesson 36

a·nach·ro·nism (ə-năk′rə-nĭz′əm) *n.* Anything out of its proper or historical time. **-a·nach′ro·nis′tic,** *adj.* **-a·nach′ro·nis′ti·cal·ly,** *adv.*

chron·ic (krŏn′ĭk) *adj.* **1.** Lasting a long time or recurring frequently. **2.** Habitual. **-chron′i·cal·ly,** *adv.*

chron·i·cle (krŏn′ĭ-kəl) *n.* A detailed record of events in the order in which they happened. *-v.* To record the history of in a chronicle.

chron·o·log·i·cal (krŏn′ə-lŏj′ĭ-kəl, krō′nə-) *adj.* Arranged in the order in which the events happened. **-chron′o·log′i·cal·ly,** *adv.*

con·tem·po·rar·y (kən-tĕm′pə-rĕr′ē) *n., pl.* **-ies.** A person who lives in the same time as another or others. *-adj.* **1.** Living at the same time. **2.** Modern.

extem·po·ra·ne·ous (ĭk-stĕm′pə-rā′nē-əs) *adj.* Done, spoken, or made with little or no preparation; impromptu. **-extem′po·ra′ne·ous·ly,** *adv.*

pro tem·po·re (prō tĕm′pə-rē) *adv.* For the time being; temporarily.

syn·chro·nize (sĭng′krə-nīz′, sĭn′-) *v.* **-nized, -niz·ing, -niz·es.** To cause to occur at the same time and together. **-syn′chro·ni·za′tion,** *n.*

tem·po·ral (tĕm′pər-əl, tĕm′prəl) *adj.* **1.** Lasting for a short time; temporary. **2.** Pertaining to life on earth; worldly.

tem·po·rize (tĕm′pə-rīz′) *v.* **-rized, -riz·ing, -riz·es. 1.** To evade action in order to gain time. **2.** To discuss in order to gain time.

Lesson 36 extemporaneous	Lesson 36 pro tempore	Lesson 36 synchronize	Lesson 36 temporal	Lesson 36 temporize
Lesson 36 anachronism	Lesson 36 chronic	Lesson 36 chronicle	Lesson 36 chronological	Lesson 36 contemporary
Lesson 35 resolute	Lesson 35 sally	Lesson 35 stalwart	Lesson 35 stamina	Lesson 35 vehement
Lesson 35 brazen	Lesson 35 dexterous	Lesson 35 incursion	Lesson 35 palpitate	Lesson 35 redoubtable
Lesson 34 interdependence	Lesson 34 intricate	Lesson 34 myriad	Lesson 34 nurture	Lesson 34 serenity
Lesson 34 anxiety	Lesson 34 appall	Lesson 34 appreciate	Lesson 34 converse	Lesson 34 economic

Word List — Red Book

Word	Lesson	Word	Lesson	Word	Lesson
aberrant	23	chronological	36	effusive	2
abject	24	claustrophobia	18	eloquent	1
abnormal	25	clemency	29	emerge	4
abridge	13	cliché	8	emissary	30
accord	9	clientele	8	emit	30
accretion	26	codify	11	empathy	18
accrue	14	cognomen	6	ensue	28
acculturate	10	collateral	14	entrée	8
acerbity	32	collide	16	entrepreneur	8
acrophobia	18	commodity	31	errant	23
adjacent	24	component	33	erratic	23
aegis	28	comport	27	eventual	13
affect	17	composite	33	evict	3
affront	32	concise	3	evince	3
agnostic	6	confound	22	exhibition	16
allegory	20	conjecture	24	exonerate	29
allusion	20	connotation	20	expedite	12
altercation	32	conscript	21	exponent	33
amnesty	28	conspiracy	25	expound	33
anachronism	36	contemporary	36	extemporaneous	36
anguish	1	contentious	32	extort	29
annals	22	contiguous	24	extract	21
annihilation	1	contingent	24	extrinsic	31
anomaly	23	continual	17	facilitate	19
antagonism	32	continuous	17	fathomless	26
anxiety	34	converge	7	feisty	22
apathy	18	converse	34	felony	29
appall	34	copious	26	ferocity	1
appreciable	26	cordial	9	finite	26
appreciate	34	countermand	12	foster	19
articulate	2	covet	31	fratricide	3
ascribe	21	creed	13	frustration	13
atmosphere	16	creep	7	galvanize	13
audit	14	culminate	7	garrulous	2
autonomy	11	culpable	29	gauche	8
avenge	17	culprit	29	gaunt	4
bedlam	5	cursive	9	generate	25
bellicose	3	cursory	9	genocide	3
belligerent	3	depict	16	glib	2
benediction	15	deportment	27	gratuitous	31
benefactor	15	desolate	7	hale	22
benevolent	15	despot	11	hallowed	31
benign	15	detract	21	harangue	1
bizarre	23	deviate	23	herculean	5
blasé	8	dexterous	35	histrionics	2
boycott	5	diagnose	6	hue	28
bravado	2	discord	9	hydrophobia	18
brazen	35	discursive	9	idiosyncratic	23
bureaucracy	11	disinterested	17	idiom	20
capital	14	disposition	33	illustrious	28
cardiac	9	dissension	32	immeasurable	13
cartel	14	diverge	7	immense	7
catastrophic	25	docile	6	impediment	12
character	13	doctrinaire	6	imperious	11
charismatic	13	doctrine	6	imply	17
charity	4	dominion	10	impostor	33
charlatan	29	duration	7	impressive	16
cherish	4	eccentricity	23	incisive	3
chronic	36	economic	34	incognito	6
chronicle	36	effect	17	incongruous	23

Word	Lesson	Word	Lesson	Word	Lesson
incorrigible	29	ostracize	32	resolute	35
incursion	35	outlandish	23	retribution	32
indefatigable	13	palpitate	35	revenge	17
indemnify	14	paltry	26	robust	10
indifference	1	paradox	6	ruse	1
indigenous	10	parody	20	ruthless	10
indoctrinate	6	pathetic	18	sally	35
induce	16	pathology	18	sanction	22
infer	17	pathos	18	sartorial	31
ingredient	16	patois	20	scourge	28
inherent	16	pecuniary	14	scripture	21
insatiable	26	pedestal	12	sedition	11
intact	24	pedigree	12	serene	22
interdependence	34	perish	4	serenity	34
intermittent	30	petition	1	shroud	4
intervene	25	pilfer	29	solecism	20
intractable	21	pittance	26	solemnity	4
intricate	34	plaintive	10	soliloquy	20
invincible	3	plethora	26	sovereign	11
iota	26	podiatrist	12	spawn	25
jargon	20	podium	12	specific	25
juxtaposition	33	polemic	2	sportive	27
kindred	25	portable	27	stalwart	35
laconic	2	portage	27	stamina	35
legion	19	portfolio	27	staunch	31
legitimate	31	portly	27	strategic	31
liquidate	14	postscript	21	structure	7
longevity	22	potpourri	8	subjective	24
lucrative	14	precursor	9	subside	4
malady	15	preeminent	22	succinct	1
malaise	15	premise	30	supposition	33
malevolence	15	prevalent	16	surpass	16
malice	4	pro tempore	36	sustain	25
malicious	15	procrustean	5	synchronize	36
malign	15	profound	19	syntax	19
malignant	15	propound	33	synthesis	10
mandate	12	prosaic	19	tact	24
mandatory	12	proscribe	21	tangent	24
manipulate	12	protract	21	tangible	24
manumit	30	psychopath	18	temporal	36
maudlin	5	pugnacious	32	temporize	36
maverick	5	purport	27	tenet	19
mentor	5	quell	10	theoretical	7
mesmerize	5	quixotic	5	totalitarian	11
metaphor	20	rancor	32	transmit	30
militant	22	rapport	27	traverse	10
minimal	25	ravage	28	trek	1
missive	30	reactionary	11	trite	2
myriad	34	recourse	9	uninterested	17
naive	8	recurrent	9	unremitting	30
nascent	19	redoubtable	35	usurp	11
nemesis	5	refine	28	usury	14
nonchalant	8	relegate	22	validate	10
nondescript	21	relentless	19	vanquish	3
novice	19	remission	30	vehement	35
nurture	34	remunerative	28	verbosity	2
omen	4	rendezvous	8	versatile	31
omission	30	renown	13	vicinity	7
opportune	27	repository	33	wield	28
orthodox	6	reprobate	29	xenophobia	18